"How I wish I had had *God's Library* when I was first—and very tentatively—introduced to the Scriptures. It would have been appreciated even more during two decades of teaching, a period during which the Hebrew and Christian Scripture's were being broken open. However, resources were scarce and one could only muddle through. Joe Paprocki's book is a small but immensely rich resource for catechist's and pastoral ministers. *God's Library* is a sure cure for what he describes as 'bibliaphobia' (a fear of the Good Book)."

Tim Unsworth
Columnist, *National Catholic Reporter*

"Joe Paprocki's *God's Library* is a critical resource for all who want to explore the Bible, but, as Mr. Paprocki acknowledges, we're afraid of it. Written in his characteristically readable style, *God's Library* offers those with no background in Scripture a rich beginning to accessing and understanding the Word of the Lord. While appropriately aimed at an adult audience, this book will entice high school and junior high people as well. The exercises invite us into the Bible; the reflection questions invite the stories of the Bible and their truth into us—our hearts and our lives. I would require *God's Library* of all those who are responsible for forming others in faith. Thanks to Mr. Paprocki, we may yet overcome the Catholic scourge of Biblical ignorance!"

Carole M. Eipers D. Min.
Director of Religious Education
Archdiocese of Chicago

"For many people, the Bible is a mysterious yet strangely familiar book. They may not know how to even begin to read it, yet there are myriad allusions to biblical data in much of the literature of western culture. People may believe that the Bible is the Book of God, but they have little or no idea of how it came to be written, or how it is put together. Such people will benefit immensely from *God's Library*.

"The book provides overviews of the biblical material; it introduces the beginner to tools for insightful readings; it explains some of the poetic expressions and exaggerations used. The author's many years in adult education make him eminently qualified to write a book that will answer many of the questions that are so often asked us."

nne Bergant, CSA
Theological Union

"For Catholics who suffer from 'bibliaphobia' Joe Paprocki's book, *God's Library* is a good way to begin to overcome the fear of reading the Bible. *God's Library* introduces the reader to the basic information needed to open the Bible and begin reading it with confidence. It will enable the reader to become familiar with the content of the Bible and the current methods of interpretation that are used to explore more deeply the meaning of biblical passages."

Pauline A. Viviano, Ph.D.
Associate Professor of Theology
Loyola University, Chicago

"*God's Library* provides a fine introduction for beginners to reading the Bible within a Catholic context. Pastors, Bible discussion leaders, DREs, and catechists have been looking for this kind of book for some time.

"*God's Library* manages to be simple without being superficial. Those who have experience in Bible study will also benefit from Joe Paprocki's witty and concise way of answering such intricate questions as 'What does the Bible really say?' and 'What's the difference between 'truth' and 'facts'?'"

Rev. John G. Lodge, S.S.L., S.T.D.
Academic Dean
Mundelein Seminary, Mundelein, IL

God's Library

Introducing Catholics
to the Bible

Joe Paprocki

TWENTY-THIRD PUBLICATIONS
Mystic, CT 06355

Acknowledgments

I would like to thank Pat Kahl for inviting me to do my first "God's Library" workshop with her wonderful sixth graders and catechists at St. Terrence in Alsip. Thanks to Regina Bajko for speedy research, Andy Bocanegra for sharing his biblical knowledge over a cheeseburger, Steve Sutera for jogging my biblical memory over breakfast, and Joanne, Mike, and Amy for loving me so much I could bust.

Special thanks to the many Scripture professors at whose feet I was privileged to sit, especially: Mark Link, SJ, Dr. Robert Ludwig, Dianne Bergant, CSA, Donald Senior, CP, Barbara Reid, OP, Eugene LaVerdiere, SSS, Leslie Hoppe, OFM, Carroll Stuhlmueller, CP, and Carolyn Osiek, RSCJ.

Second printing 2000

Twenty-Third Publications/Bayard
185 Willow Street
P.O. Box 180
Mystic, CT 06355
(860) 536-2611
(800) 321-0411

ISBN: 0-89622-970-X
Library of Congress Catalog Card Number: 98-61773
Printed in the U.S.A.

Dedication

I dedicate this book to the late Sr. Georgine Smolinski, CR, who firmly believed that a teenager could possibly be interested in the Bible and to Fr. Terry Baum, SJ, for giving that teenager spiritual direction that has lasted a lifetime.

Table of Contents

God's Library

ONE

Overcoming "Bibliaphobia"

In the famous cartoon *A Charlie Brown Christmas,* Charlie seeks the advice of his friend Lucy, explaining that he just doesn't feel right. Charlie listens as Lucy goes through a long list of phobias that might possibly explain Charlie's problem, including fears of responsibility, cats, staircases, the ocean, and crossing bridges. Finally, Lucy suggests that perhaps Charlie's problem is being caused by something called *pantaphobia.* When Lucy explains that *pantaphobia* is the fear of EVERYTHING, Charlie shouts, *"That's it!"*

As a catechist or pastoral minister, you, too, have some fears. I hope you are not suffering from *pantaphobia* like Charlie Brown, but many things about teaching the faith can indeed be frightening. Among some of the fears that I've "diagnosed" in catechists and pastoral ministers over the years are the following:

Adolescentaphobia: fear of teaching junior high

Disciplinariaphobia: fear of discipline problems in our classes

Artsandcraftsaphobia: fear of anything to do with cutting and pasting

DREaphobia: fear of our Director of Religious Education

Pastoraphobia: fear of our pastor

1

One fear, however, is very common among Catholic catechists and pastoral ministers. It is a fear I call *bibliaphobia* (*biblia* = Bible; *phobia* = fear of)—fear of the Bible. Let's face it, many of us have a fear of the Good Book. As Catholics, many of us were not encouraged (and in many cases were discouraged) when it came to the idea of reading or studying the Bible. We were told to let Father explain it to us on Sunday. Even though Vatican II stressed the importance of becoming familiar with the Bible, reading and reflecting on the Scriptures on our own, it has been hard to shake the notion that Scripture study was something that the Protestants did. As a result, many of us still feel at a loss when it comes to understanding—let alone explaining—the Bible to others. We fear the topic of the Bible coming up in conversation. We feel intimidated by many of our Protestant brothers and sisters who can quote chapter and verse. Most of all, we have no idea what to tell our students or our children when they ask, "Is it *true* that Noah built an ark or Adam lived to be 930 years old or Jonah was swallowed by a whale?" What do we say? How do we answer such questions? What do we believe for ourselves?

"I Was Never Taught to Read the Bible..."

For many of us, the Bible was a very large book kept on a shelf in the living room or dining room, and used mainly as a place to record the family history. It was less a book to read and more of a relic to store in the house, a sacramental that reminded us of the presence of God's Word in the home. As children, many of us encountered the Bible only when we had pasted some pictures on a poster for a school project and needed something heavy to press them down overnight. Rare was the occasion that this great big book was pulled out to be read from. For one thing, it was too heavy. For another, it had words that sounded strange and foreign…too many "thee's" and "thou's" for our liking. More important, many of us were simply not encouraged to read the Bible. Some Catholics actually recall being discouraged from reading the Bible in the days before Vatican II.

"Bible Study is a Protestant Thing."

One reason Catholics shied away from the Bible was because we viewed the Bible as a Protestant thing. Suspicious of the axiom "Scripture alone," seen as a battle cry for Protestants, Catholics kept the Bible at arm's length, trusting the hierarchy, the nuns, and our CCD teachers to sort out the Bible messages intended for our ears. As long as we had the Sacraments, Tradition, and Father's homily, we had little reason to sit down and read the Bible privately, let alone attempt to interpret the Word of God.

The Underlying Causes of Bibliaphobia

Most phobias are an exaggerated or irrational fear, dread, or aversion to any object or stimulus. In most cases, there may indeed be something to fear, but the fear becomes out of proportion or irrational. *Bibliaphobia* works much the same way. While it is true that there are some things about the Bible that may be intimidating, many of us avoid it as though it were a swarm of bees. Let's take a look at some aspects of the Bible that may be intimidating and add to our *bibliaphobia.*

•"It's too long." Most of us are accustomed to reading books that have fairly good size print and are about 200-300 pages in length. The Bible, on the other hand, usually has very tiny print, and contains anywhere between 1000 and 2500 pages, depending on which version we're reading

• "It has too many names I don't recognize." Eldad, Medad, Meshach, Shadrach, Abednego, Zephaniah, Zechariah, Caiaphas, Annas, etc. Who *are* these people? So and so begot so and so who begot so and so…these names don't ring any bells for us at first glance.

• "It has too many places I've never heard of." Marah, Elim, Rephidim, Shiloh, Samaria, Colossus, Thessalonica…even the letter to the Philippians has nothing to do with the Philippines. Where *are* these places? It's hard to understand a story if we don't understand the setting.

• "It uses images that don't belong to our time and culture." We live in an age of computer chips, cellular phones, websites, and DVD-TV. References to shekels, cubits, sheep, arks, nets, and mustard seeds often leave us scratching our heads.

• "It's not like other books." Most books have a beginning, middle, and an end, divided up into chapters. The Bible, on the other hand has testaments, books, chapters, and verses. Most books are chronological. The Bible seems to jump around a lot.

• "Some of the stories just seem incredible." Most of us have never seen burning bushes, parting seas, arks, talking serpents, or people swallowed by whales. It's hard to understand these stories when we have no common frame of reference.

• "You need to be a Scripture scholar to interpret the Bible." The Bible seems to be so complex and contains so many layers of meaning that most of us feel inept and inadequate when it comes to making biblical interpretations. It feels like you need to study a whole semester of graduate theology just to understand a few passages.

• "I don't know anything about Judaism...but that's all the Old Testament talks about." Most of us are struggling just to be good Christians. The Bible, on the other hand—especially the Old Testament (which is three-fourths of the entire Bible)—seems to require a great deal of knowledge about the Jewish faith and way of life.

• "I honestly don't know if I can stomach some of it." Jesus talks about loving enemies, praying for persecutors, turning the other cheek, how blessed it is to be poor, and dying in order to live. How do we live these ideas today? Can we?

• "I could never quote chapter and verse like many Protestants can." On TV and in life, we see so many preachers, ministers, and ordinary people, most often Protestant, who can quote the Bible from memory, citing chapter and verse. Do we need to learn the Bible that way too? Many of us are not sure if we can or even want to.

Having noted all of these common fears and concerns about the Bible, perhaps I have confirmed your notion that the Bible *is* something to shy away from. On the contrary, I am just pointing out that these fears and concerns about the Bible are not yours alone. They are shared by many people, especially Catholics who have not had much Bible exposure and experience. With some common sense understanding of the Bible, how it is put together, and how we are to read and interpret it, these fears and concerns can easily be overcome. Like any phobia, fear of the Bible is overcome by facing up to the seemingly overwhelming obstacles and learning to see them in a whole new way while removing the fear.

Symptoms of Bibliaphobia

So, how can you tell if you're suffering from *bibliaphobia*? Like any other phobia, there are very clear symptoms that can be detected. Use the following checklist to determine your level of *bibliaphobia*. Apply the following ratings to each item:

0 = Totally Disagree
1 = Somewhat Disagree
2 = Somewhat Agree
3 = Totally Agree

_____ You have trouble locating even famous Bible stories and characters

_____ You shy away from discussions about the Bible

_____ You feel intimidated by those you feel have more Bible knowledge

_____ You have difficulty answering questions your children ask about the Bible

_____ You rarely attempt reading the Bible on your own

_____ You feel inadequate when it comes to the idea of attending Bible study

_____ Locating a passage identified by book, chapter, and verse (e.g. 1 Pt 2:3) seems more difficult than solving an algebra problem

_____ After reading a Bible passage, you often feel you have no idea what it meant

_____ You find many Bible stories confusing

_____ Your Bible is still in store-bought "mint" condition

Now, add up your total score and determine your level of *bibliaphobia:*

Your Total: _____ Check the category below that fits your score.

___ 0 = None   (You're perfectly at home with the Bible)
___ 1-10 = Mild   (The Bible presents some challenges to you)
___ 11-20 = Moderate   (You find the Bible to be most difficult)
___ 21-29 = Severe   (You have a strong fear of the Bible)
___ 30 = BIBLIAPHOBIA ALERT   (You need Bible therapy)

Acknowledging the problem

Our lack of knowledge about the Bible can often be an embarrassment. How can we, adult Catholic Christians, admit to not knowing or understanding the Word of God? We may not even realize how inadequate our understanding of the Bible really is until we are put to the test.

Did someone say a test? What a great idea.

Before we go any further, take the B.A.T. test (the Bible Awareness Test) to see just how familiar (or unfamiliar) you are with the Bible and its contents.

The B.A.T. (Bible Awareness Test)

Try to locate the following Bible passages one at a time in under 2 minutes each:

• David and Goliath

• Noah's Ark

• Jonah and the Whale

• Moses crossing the Red Sea

• Daniel in the lion's den

• Zacchaeus the tax collector

• Jesus walking on the water

• Pentecost

• Hg 2:1–3

• The Second Book of Chronicles, chapter 29, verses nine to fifteen

Now, add up your score of how many Bible passages you were able to locate in under 2 minutes each and determine your BQ (Bible Quotient):

Your BQ (Bible Quotient)

10	High: You probably don't need this book.
7-9	Average: Not bad but keep reading.
3-8	Fair: This book is required reading.
0-2	Low: You *need* this book.

This very unscientific test is only an indicator of how familiar or unfamiliar you are with the Bible. However, the reason we are not familiar with the Bible is because we do not understand it and, as a result, we fear it. We always tend to fear the things we are most unfamiliar with. We can overcome our fears of the Bible by becoming more familiar with the Good Book. Paradoxically, we will become more familiar with the Bible by overcoming our fears of it. Don't let *bibliaphobia* get the best of you. Don't become the "Charlie Brown" of catechists or pastoral ministers...paralyzed by an irrational fear that prevents you from discovering the meaning of life that we discover in reading the Bible.

And Now, the Good News!

The good news (aside from the gospel of Jesus Christ) is that, with a few tips and some practice, reading and understanding the Bible can become much easier and extremely fulfilling. The Bible was not written for scholars, it was written for you and me. The Bible is God speaking to you and me in the course of human events. It is meant to be read not only in churches and universities, but on subways, at bus stops, in the cafeteria, in your rocking chair, in bed, or listened to on tape or CD as you drive. Sure, certain aspects of the Bible may seem intimidating, but when you stop to think about the fact that the Creator of the Universe has something to say to *you*, it makes the notion of learning about the Bible a little bit more enticing.

The Bible has been a powerful influence in my own experience and in the experience of countless numbers of people. It is not only the story of people who lived thousands of years ago. It is the story of *your* life and *my* life. Every Bible story is a metaphor for the many experiences of God we have all had and will have in our lives. So, as we prepare to look at burning bushes, parting seas, calmings of storms, healings of the blind, deaf, and paralyzed, and raisings from the dead, know that somehow, these experiences are part of the story of your life and my life.

Welcome to God's Library!

Overcoming *bibliaphobia* is a matter of changing one's perception of the object or stimulus supposedly causing the fear. The first thing we need to change when considering the Bible is our perception of the Bible as a *book*. It really isn't a book at all! The word *biblia* comes from the Greek

9

meaning "books." In reality, the Bible is a *collection* of books—73 in all. For that reason, I prefer to think of the Bible as God's Library. What is a library other than a collection of books brought together in one place for the reader to gain access to? When we understand the Bible as God's Library, it changes our approach to how we are to read and understand its writings. We would never go to a library assuming that we are supposed to begin reading the first book on the first shelf and progress to the last book on the last shelf. Nor would we suppose that all of the books in a library are meant to be understood in exactly the same way or that all are the same type of literature. Once we learn how to "use" a library, we are capable of accessing the power of its contents. In the same way, once we learn how to "use" God's Library, the Bible, we will be able to access the mighty power of *its* contents.

So, welcome to God's Library. Leave your *bibliaphobia* at the door and enter into a collection of writings about how God powerfully lives and moves in the lives of some very interesting people...including *you*.

Questions for Reflection and Discussion

•What has your experience of the Bible been...as a child...teen...young adult...presently?

•What do you find most intimidating about the Bible?

•What do you find most attractive or inviting about the Bible?

•Who is someone you know that knows the Bible extremely well? Where did he/she get their knowledge of the Bible from?

•How would a better understanding of the Bible make a difference in your life and/or ministry?

•What is the one thing you need to improve at the most when it comes to knowing or understanding the Bible?

•How have you used libraries in your life? Describe how libraries "work" and keep this description handy as you continue reading this book. Apply these concepts to God's Library, the Bible.

TWO

Welcome to God's Library

Imagine that the following lines are taken from someone's personal journal or diary as they set out to read the entire Bible from cover to cover:

DAY ONE: O.K. I'm finally going to do it. I'm going to read the Bible from start to finish. I've got my classical music…my reading glasses…a candle…my slippers…a cozy rocking chair, and a snack. If I stick to it, I can do this in about a month or two.

DAY FOUR: So far, so good. Genesis isn't too bad. Some very interesting stories. A few too many genealogies. Too many directions for building the ark…what's a cubit, anyway? Good characters. All in all, I'm off to a good start.

DAY SIX: Exodus is even better than Genesis. I love those Moses stories. I remember them from my childhood. Can't beat the ten plagues and the parting of the Red Sea for drama. Gets a little bogged down after the Ten Commandments. Still, I'm doing it. Two books down and 71 to go.

DAY FIFTEEN: What happened? I was doing pretty well. Then came Leviticus. I can hardly keep my eyes open. Laws…rules…directions…penalties…it's all so tedious. I'll just have to bear down and get through it.

DAY THIRTY: I thought the book of Numbers would be better...I was wrong.

DAY SIXTY: I've been kind of busy lately...I'll get through this eventually. I'll get back into reading. It's got to get better. I think I left off in the book of Judges.

DAY ONE HUNDRED: Well...at least I tried.

The Problems Begin On Page One

Many of us can relate to the above fictional journal entries. We want to read the Bible and we set forth determined to conquer it, only to give up after a while, concluding that the Bible is a book written for scholars, not for ordinary folk like us. The problem lies in the fact that we approach the Bible the way we approach any other book...we start on page one and hope to get to the last page some day. Even humongous tomes such as *War and Peace* can be conquered using this basic method of reading cover to cover. However, the Bible is no ordinary book. As we said, it is a collection of books, a library. Sure, the Bible *can* be read from cover to cover; many have done so with great delight. However, many others have tried and failed, only to miss out on the powerful message of God's Word. The Bible is a collection of books brought together into one place so that God's Word can be at our fingertips—only a few feet from our minds and hearts. If we are going to approach the Bible, we need to approach it as if we were climbing the steps to enter a library building. Like any library, it makes available to us a rich variety of readings from which we may choose selections for various occasions and purposes. So, instead of thinking of the Bible as a book to finish from cover to cover, approach it instead as a library to become more familiar with over time. The more familiar you become with God's Library, the more you will use it. The more you use it, the more of it you will read and understand. The more you read and understand it, the closer you will be to the God who speaks to you in and through it.

How a Library Works
Knowing that the Bible can be understood as God's Library, perhaps we should spend some time making a comparison to a typical library and see how a trip to the local library can teach us a few things about how to "use" the Bible.

Over the course of our lives, most of us have made numerous trips to various libraries in our schools and communities. We go for various reasons: research, recreation, enrichment, entertainment, escape, peace and quiet, etc. How do we "use" a library? It's easy. For most of us, it entails the following:

•Check the catalogue for assistance in locating the author or book title

•locate the section of the library in which that type of literature (or the book's assigned number) can be found

•locate the item(s) you are interested in reading

•check out the item(s)

•take the item(s) home and read at your leisure or as needed

In other words, there's nothing too mysterious about using a library.

What About God's Library?
Since the Bible is God's library, it makes sense that we

would use it in much the same way. We come to God's library for many reasons: research, prayer, inspiration, curiosity, enjoyment, encouragement, etc. We also come to it with different tastes. Some of us prefer the psalms and the proverbs over the letters and the parables. What we find when we enter God's library is an arrangement not unlike the one we just described. In fact, we find the following:

•a "catalogue": the Table of Contents and Indices

•2 large "halls" or "wings": the Old and New Testaments (also known as the Hebrew and Christian Scriptures)

•smaller sections or "stack rooms" within these 2 great halls: Pentateuch (or Torah), History, Wisdom, Prophets, Gospels, Acts, Letters, and Revelation

In fact, if the Bible were truly a library building, its set-up might look something like this:

Old Testament	Catalog	New Testament
Pentateuch (Torah)	*Table of Contents*	**Gospels**
History		**Acts**
Wisdom		**Letters**
Prophets		**Revelation**

Let's take a closer look now at the various parts of God's Library.

Using the "Catalogue"

Nowadays, most library catalogues are on computer. However, the basic idea has not changed. Titles of authors and books are arranged in alphabetical order for easy reference and locating. Many of us are guilty of ignoring the catalogue at the library and heading straight for the shelves in an attempt to find a certain book or two. More often than not, we end up searching aisle after aisle and shelf after shelf with little or no luck. In much the same way, many of us attempt to locate passages in the Bible without using the "catalogue" at the front called the Table of Contents or Index. In the Table of Contents, you will more than likely find the following:

• an outline of the books of the Bible in the order in which they appear (Old Testament and New Testament) as well as the page number

• an alphabetical listing of the same

• an alphabetical listing of abbreviations of each book

A typical Table of Contents page in a typical Bible will look something like this:

OLD TESTAMENT (HEBREW SCRIPTURES)

Book	Abbreviation	Page
Genesis	Gn	1
Exodus	Ex	50
Leviticus	Lv	100
Numbers	Nm	130
Deuteronomy	Dt	170

...and so on, listing all 46 Old Testament books. See the Appendix for the complete list—or pick up a Bible and check it out for yourself.

In the same way, the New Testament (Christian Scriptures) listing would look like this:

NEW TESTAMENT (CHRISTIAN SCRIPTURES)

Book	Abbreviation	Page
Matthew	Mt	1000
Mark	Mk	1050
Luke	Lk	1075
John	Jn	1115

...and so on, listing all 27 of the New Testament books. (Some Bibles begin the pagination of the New Testament by going back to page 1.)

A separate *alphabetical* listing may also be found in your Table of Contents section. It might look something like this:

OLD TESTAMENT (HEBREW SCRIPTURES)

Book	Abbreviation	Page
Amos	Am	900
Baruch	Bar	875
1 Chronicles	1 Chr	350
2 Chronicles	2 Chr	400
Daniel	Dn	950

...and so on.

The New Testament (Christian Scriptures) would look like this:

NEW TESTAMENT (CHRISTIAN SCRIPTURES)

Book	Abbreviation	Page
Acts of the Apostles	Acts	1200
Colossians	Col	1300
1 Corinthians	1 Cor	1250

| 2 Corinthians | 2 Cor | 1275 |
| Ephesians | Eph | 1290 |

...and so on. For a complete listing of the contents of the Bible, see the Appendix of this book, page 108.

Now that we see how the Bible's catalogue is arranged, let's take a closer look at how to use it.

Is it "Judg." "Jg." or "Jgs."?

Learning to use the abbreviation page of your Bible is crucial to being able to locate Bible passages. One thing to be aware of, however, is the fact that not all Bibles abbreviate books in the same way. A little later on, we'll discuss the differences between various Bibles and how to choose one, but for now, suffice it to say that one of the differences is the variety of abbreviations used to refer to the same book. For example, the book of Judges can be found abbreviated as Judg., Jg., or Jgs., depending on which Bible translation you are looking at. Knowing that Bibles abbreviate books differently will help avoid a great deal of confusion down the line, especially if you are in a group of people using a variety of Bible translations/editions.

The Bible's Book Numbering System

In any catalogue, you need to understand how to use the book numbering system to locate the book you're looking for on the shelves. The same is true of locating passages in God's Library. No, the Bible does not use the Dewey Decimal system or the Library of Congress classification system, but instead has its own system of identifying books, chapters, and verses. It's called Scripture citation. You've seen it before. It looks like this:

1 Pt 2:1–4

Unfortunately, to some of us, this may very well look as complicated as a trigonometry equation. Until we know how to decipher Scripture citation, we will have very little luck locating Scripture passages by book, chapter, and verse. The key to understanding Scripture citation is really quite simple. It always follows this format:

Name of the Book   Chapter   colon   verse   hyphen   verse

1 Pt (1 Peter)   2   :   1   –   4

By using your table of contents (namely the abbreviation page and the alphabetical listing, you would be able to decipher 1 Pt 2:1–4 as:

The first letter of Peter, chapter two, verses one to four.

Here are a few more examples:

Jgs 15:6–15   *The book of Judges, chapter fifteen, verses six to fifteen*

Zep 3:18–19   *The book of Zephaniah, chapter three, verses eighteen to nineteen*

Jn 7:3–6,10   *The Gospel of John, chapter seven, verses three to six and verse ten*

Ti 2:11–14   *The letter to Titus, chapter two, verses eleven to fourteen*

Now, try some on your own for practice. If you need help with the abbreviations, use your own Bible's Table of Contents or see pg. 108 of the Appendix in this book:

Is 42:5–10_____

Hg 3:6–11_____

1 Mac 6:1–6_____

3 Jn 1:2–4_____

Jas 2:7–9_____

Mk 9:8–15_____

*Answer key: Isaiah chapter forty two, verses five to ten; Haggai chapter three, verses six to eleven; First book of Maccabees chapter six, verses one to six; Third letter of John chapter one, verses two to four; Letter of James chapter two, verses seven to nine; Mark chapter nine, verses eight to fifteen.

Now, try the same thing in reverse order: take the following passages described in *prose* and write them in *citation* form. The first one is done as an example:

The book of Daniel, chapter four, verse eleven:
Dn 4:11

The letter to the Romans, chapter five, verses three to six:

_____

The book of Judith, chapter two, verses nine to sixteen:

_____

The book of Habakkuk, chapter three, verse twelve:

_____

The Gospel of Matthew, chapter five, verses one to nine:

_____

* Answer Key: Dn 4:11; Rom 5:3–6; Jdt 2:9–16; Hab 3:12; Mt 5:1–9

Once you have mastered the skill of Scripture citation using the Table of Contents and Index, you are well on your way to locating Scripture passages in just a matter of moments.

Now that you know how to locate passages when you are looking for a particular book, chapter, and verse, let's turn to how you can locate a particular *story* in the Bible when you have no idea what book it is in. That's another skill that can be learned using some simple steps.

Bookmarks and Training Wheels

Think back to when you learned how to ride a two-wheeler. More than likely, you used training wheels until you developed your own sense of balance. After much practice, the training wheels eventually came off and you were on your way. In the same way, we are going to look at a simple skill (involving bookmarks) that can be used like training wheels until you develop your own sense of how to maneuver through the Bible.

What happens when you want to find the story of David and Goliath...Solomon building the Temple...Jacob and Esau...Zacchaeus...the conversion of Saul...the last supper...and you don't know what book they are in? How does one go about developing a familiarity with the Bible that allows for quick location of such wonderful and famous stories and characters? In the Appendix of this book, you will find nine bookmarks (pp. 113-117). Copy these on heavy stock and cut along the lines and get ready to learn the answer to these questions.

Recall our diagram of God's Library on page 15. Keep it handy as a quick reference as we maneuver through the nooks and crannies of the Bible. First and foremost, we need to state the obvious: the Bible is divided into two

21

parts…the Old Testament (Hebrew Scriptures) and the New Testament (Christian Scriptures)—or the First Testament and the Second Testament..

• Let's begin by separating our Bibles into these two parts

• Using your Table of Contents, locate the last page of the book of Malachi which is the last page of the Old Testament.

• Now, find the first page of the New Testament (the gospel of Matthew).

• Place your bookmark (Appendix pg. 117) here to separate the Old and New Testaments.

• Now, take a look at how the Bible is separated. Observe how large the Old Testament is in comparison to the New Testament.

• Keep in mind the clearest and most simple distinction between the Old and New Testaments:

• The Old Testament is the story of the people of Israel *before* the birth of Jesus Christ.

• The New Testament is the story of the *Christian* experience, beginning with the life of Jesus Christ and continuing with the early church

Once you have this clear distinction in your head, you will have a clearer understanding of where to begin searching for stories in the Bible by asking yourself one simple question: is this story directly related to the life of Jesus and the early church? If the answer is *yes*, then you'll be looking in the New Testament. If not, you'll be searching through the Old Testament. "Great," you may be saying, "but I still have to sift through a thousand pages to find the story I'm looking for." This is true, but what we are about to do is to break the Bible down into smaller sections. For starters, we have divided the Bible into two very large sections. Now that we've done so, get the rest of your bookmarks ready and let's see how each Testament can be broken down even further into four smaller units and what can be found within each of them. The following outlines (also found on the bookmarks) can be seen as brief introductory summaries of the highlights (not a complete concordance) of each section of the Bible. By using the bookmarks and the highlights outline, you can have easy access to the various parts of the Bible.

God's Library Highlights (Old Testament)

Select the four bookmarks for the Old Testament (see Appendix pp. 113-114) or cut out four bookmarks of one color if the Appendix bookmarks are unavailable.

PENTATEUCH (Torah): The first five books of the Old Testament (Genesis through Deuteronomy)

Place the "Pentateuch" (Pen-tuh-tuke) bookmark on the last page of the book of Deuteronomy. The pages from the beginning of Genesis to this bookmark make up the section called "Pentateuch" (called Torah in the Hebrew Scriptures), meaning the five books of the Law. This section captures the beginnings of the relationship between God and the people of Israel with the central focus being the Exodus event...the experience of being led from slavery to freedom. Here are some of the highlights:

•the creation stories

•Adam and Eve

•Cain and Abel

•Noah's ark

•The tower of Babel

•Sodom and Gomorrah

•Abraham and Sarah

•Isaac and Rebekah

•Jacob and Esau

•Joseph (the "coat of many colors")

•Moses (in the reeds, the burning bush, the ten plagues, crossing of the Red Sea, the Passover, the ten commandments, the ark of the covenant, journey through the desert, death of Moses)

•the twelve tribes of Israel

•the laws, traditions, and feasts of Israel

HISTORY: (Joshua through 2 Maccabees)

Place the bookmark entitled "History" on the last page of 2 Maccabees. The section from the "Pentateuch" bookmark to this bookmark makes up the History section of God's Library. This section records the story of the people of Israel fighting to establish and keep the promised land under various leaders (judges and kings). Here are the highlights:

•Joshua (crossing the Jordan, the walls of Jericho)

• Samson and Delilah

• Ruth and Naomi

• Samuel (request for a king)

• King Saul

• David and Goliath, King David

• Solomon (the Temple, Queen of Sheba)

• Elijah and Elisha

• many kings, battles, and genealogies

• division of the kingdom

• exile and return

• Judith and Esther

WISDOM: (Job through Sirach)

Place the bookmark named "Wisdom" at the end of the book of Sirach (or Ecclesiasticus, as it is called in some Bibles). You're now ready to explore the Wisdom section of the Bible: everything from the "History" bookmark to this bookmark. While the Bible is full of wisdom, this particular section gathers together all the wisdom teachings of the people of Israel collected over thousands of years of wandering the desert, living in the promised land, worshiping in the temple, and struggling through exile. There are many anecdotes, sayings, prayers, poems, and songs in the Wisdom books. Here are some highlights:

• Job's suffering

• 150 Psalms for all occasions

•hundreds of proverbs

•wise sayings including "Vanity of vanities, all things are vanity" and "There is a time for everything" and "A faithful friend is a sturdy shelter" and more

•a romantic love song (Song of Songs, or Song of Solomon)

•thousands more sayings about wisdom, prudence, good health, wealth, holiness, family, friends, misery, death, and even table etiquette.

PROPHETS: (Isaiah through Malachi)
Place the last of your four Old Testament bookmarks, titled "Prophets," at the end of the book of Malachi (which also coincides with the bookmark separating the Old and New Testaments). Welcome to the last section of the Old Testament: the Prophets (everything from your "Wisdom" bookmark to this one). The prophets were not concerned with foretelling the future. Their purpose was to call the people of Israel to return to their past fidelity to God, lest they face doom. Likewise, when the people of Israel found themselves doomed in exile, the prophets held out hope for the future. From this hope comes the notion of a messiah and an everlasting kingdom. Yet even these assurances of a future are based on a return to the fidelity of the past. Here are some highlights:

•The "major" (lengthier) prophets:

> Isaiah (Immanuel, "the people who walked in darkness have seen a great light," "comfort my people," etc.)

> Jeremiah (call of Jeremiah, exile and return)

Ezekiel (the dry bones)

•The "minor" (shorter) prophets including:

Daniel (the lion's den, Shadrach, Meshach, and Abednego),

Jonah (swallowed by a whale)

...and more.

God's Library Highlights (New Testament)

Use the four New Testament bookmarks (see Appendix pg. 115-116) or cut out four bookmarks of one color (different from the Old Testament color) if the Appendix is unavailable.

GOSPELS: (Matthew, Mark, Luke, and John)

Place the "Gospels" bookmark at the end of the gospel of John and prepare to enter the part of God's Library where we walk with Jesus: the beginning of the New Testament up to this bookmark. The gospels (Matthew, Mark, Luke, and John) contain the stories that are most sacred to our Christian faith and heritage: the life, teachings, miracles, passion, death, and resurrection of Jesus of Nazareth. If you're looking for a story about Jesus, this is the place to look. Here are some highlights:

•the birth of Jesus (the Magi, the shepherds, etc.)

•the Holy Family (Mary and Joseph)

•the finding in the temple

•temptation in the desert and the baptism of Jesus

•the Beatitudes and the Our Father

•parables (the prodigal son, the good samaritan, the sower, the mustard seed, etc.)

•the golden rule and the great commandment

•numerous miracles (calming of the storm, healing of the blind, deaf, and paralyzed, raising of Lazarus, changing water into wine, feeding 5000, walking on water, etc.)

•the last supper, Eucharist, and the washing of the feet

•the agony in the garden

•Peter's denial and Judas' betrayal

•the way of the cross

•Crucifixion

•Resurrection and appearances

•dozens of fascinating characters: Zacchaeus, Pontius Pilate, Mary Magdalene, Nicodemus, the Samaritan woman, Martha and Mary, etc.

•powerful images such as the Bread of Life, the Light of the World, the Way, Truth, and the Life

ACTS OF THE APOSTLES: (One book only)
This section of the Bible is easy because it is just one book: the Acts of the Apostles. Place the bookmark titled "Acts" at the end of this book and visit the experience of the early Christian community. In many ways, the book of Acts is a sequel to the gospels, especially the gospel of Luke, since Luke and Acts were written by the same author. Here are some highlights of Acts:

• Jesus' ascension

• the descent of the Holy Spirit on Pentecost

• descriptions of the communal life of the early church

• Stephen's martyrdom

• Philip and the Ethiopian

• Saul's conversion and baptism

• the missionary work of Peter, Saul (Paul), Barnabas, and others

• miracles at the hands of Peter and Paul

• Paul's travels, imprisonment, trials, shipwreck, and arrival in Rome

THE LETTERS (Epistles): (Romans through Jude)
Place the "Letters" bookmark at the end of the letter of Jude. Everything from the "Acts" bookmark up to this one represents the communications of the early church, before e-mail, phones, and FAXes. The majority (12) of the 21 letters, also known as epistles, are attributed to Paul. These letters are addressed to communities of Christians and to the leaders of these communities and were designed to teach, admonish, encourage, correct, and update the various churches. Here are some highlights:

• **Paul**: theology, teachings, and exhortations concerning:

• grace

• justification by faith

• the Law

- the Eucharist

- the metaphor of the Body

- variety and unity of gifts

- ministry

- suffering

- Christ and his cross

- Christian conduct

James: faith and good works, anointing of the sick

1 John: "Beloved, let us love one another..."

REVELATION: (One book only)

Place your last bookmark (named "Revelation") at the end of the book of Revelation, and you've reached the end of the Bible. As you enter the book of Revelation, be aware that it is one of the most misunderstood books of the Bible. Many falsely use this book to predict the end of the world. Written in "apocalyptic" language, the book of Revelation uses many symbols and figurative language to describe the eternal struggle between good and evil. Despite all of the frightening imagery, the uplifting conclusion of this book is that good has and always will prevail. Here are the highlights:

- visions and messages to the seven churches

- the scroll and the lamb

- the 144,000 saved

- the seven trumpets

•the woman and the dragon

•the King of Kings

•the Thousand-Year Reign

•the new heavens and new earth

•the new Jerusalem

•"Come, Lord Jesus"

Practicing With Your "Training Wheels"

Now that your bookmarks are in place, practice locating some of the highlights outlined on them or from the previous few pages. Browse through a section of God's Library searching for some of the famous characters and stories. Don't set out to read whole sections. For now, just browse around until you discover passages that you are particularly interested in reading right now. If you don't understand a section or the reading is becoming tedious and difficult to understand, move on.

As you become more and more skilled at Bible reading, you can return to these more difficult and challenging sections. There are many other books about the Bible available to assist you at that next level. For now, focus on getting to know the sections of the Bible as well as a flavor for what can be found in each section. Most important, use your bookmarks to become more familiar with where these various sections of the Bible are. Your bookmarks will act as training wheels for the time being, assisting you in traversing the terrain of the Bible. Eventually, however, the training wheels must come off. When you feel you have worked hard at getting to know the locations of the various sections of the Bible, remove your bookmarks and continue trying to locate passages, stories, and characters in their respective sections. It may still take you some time to locate certain specific passages. However, you will have a much greater chance of speeding up the time in which you do so because you will be in the right "ballpark," so to speak. Try doing the following exercise as a way of developing your God's Library skills.

God's Library Exercise

Determine which section of God's Library the following stories and characters may be found in by matching the following selections with one of the 8 sections of the Bible.

a. Pentateuch b. History c. Wisdom d. Prophets

e. Gospels f. Acts g. Letters h. Revelation

___ 1. Solomon's Temple

___ 2. The Seventh Trumpet

___ 3. Jonah and the whale

___ 4. Saul's conversion

___ 5. Noah's ark

___ 6. Jacob and Esau

___ 7. The scriptural way of the cross

___ 8. Stephen's martyrdom

___ 9. Paul writing to the people of Ephesus

___ 10. The New Jerusalem

___ 11. David and Goliath

___ 12. Moses and the burning bush

___ 13. Zacchaeus

___ 14. The raising of Lazarus

___ 15. The dry bones

___ 16. Joseph and the "coat of many colors"

___ 17. Justification by faith

___ 18. The Holy Spirit on Pentecost

___ 19. Samson and Delilah

___ 20. The Ten Commandments

Answer Key: 1. b 2. h 3. d 4. f 5. a 6. a 7. e 8. f 9. g 10. h 11. b 12. a 13. e 14. e 15. d 16. a 17. g 18. f 19. b 20. a

Questions for Reflection and Discussion

• Which Bible stories do you have the most trouble locating?

• Did you ever try to read the Bible cover to cover? What was your experience?

• How can you compare the Bible to a library?

• What can be compared to a "catalogue" in God's Library? How do we use it?

• In what ways can the Table of Contents and Index pages of your Bible assist you in your prayer life? In your Bible study?

• What are the eight sections of God's Library? Can you briefly summarize what and who can be found in each?

• How can breaking the Bible down into these eight sections help you in your knowledge and familiarity of the Bible?

• As a result of practicing using your bookmarks, what section of the Bible are you discovering for the first time?

• What section of the Bible do you look forward to getting to know better? Why?

THREE

The Bible as a Time Capsule

What Is It? What Does It Mean?

Some years ago, Pepsi ran a television commercial that took place in a futuristic setting with a professor leading a group of students on an archeological dig. As they all drink from their Pepsi cans, one of them unearths a find; an object caked over with centuries of mud and dirt. Unable to make out what the object is, the professor places it in a device that quickly removes all of the layers of dirt only to reveal an empty bottle of Coca Cola. With puzzled expressions, all of the students look at the object and ask the professor, "What is it?" The professor, with the same puzzled expression tilts the bottle this way and that before responding, "I have *no idea!*"

This clever commercial attempted to show us how something that once was a familiar sight and a household name can fade from memory over a long period of time and become so anachronistic that no one can identify it or make sense out of it. Pepsi and Coca Cola can fight this one out over the next few centuries. For our purposes, the point is well taken and can be applied to our exploration of God's Library. Much of the Bible, written centuries ago, is as foreign to many of us as that Coca Cola bottle appeared to be to those students in the commercial. Characters, places, phrases, stories, and words that were easily identified and understood by the people of biblical times can be frustratingly strange to people of the twenty-first century. Quite often, when we read a segment of God's Library, we react in the same way the students in the commercial reacted, by asking, "What is it? What does it mean?" Like the professor, we too unfortunately often come to the conclusion that, "I have *no idea!*"

Knowing where things are and how they can be found in God's Library was the first skill to learn in overcoming our *bibliaphobia.* Now, we have to face up to the daunting task of trying to understand what it is that we are reading. For many of us, once we get past the challenge of locating a story, our joy is short-lived because as we enter into the passage, we find that we are dealing with material that was written long ago in a land far away from our back porch. Our satisfaction at locating a passage often turns to frustration when we realize that we have little or no idea of what we just read or how to properly understand it. Like a student browsing through a library, we need help not only in locating what we want to read, but in understanding the material we are reading. We need some assistance in accessing and unleashing the power of God's Word. For many of us, this Word may seem buried under centuries of dirt, clay, and dried mud, preventing us from applying it to our present-day experience.

So far, our primary metaphor for the Bible is that of a library. Another helpful metaphor I would like to suggest is that of a *time capsule.*

The Bible as a Time Capsule

We all know what a time capsule is and how it works. People gather objects that capture the essence and experience of their particular time and place and put them into a container. The container may contain objects that convey the mood of the times, the fads, the defining moments, the culture, the customs, the famous people, the music, the headlines, the milestones, the accomplishments, and much more. When all of the objects are gathered into the container, it is sealed and buried or placed somewhere with the idea that it will not be unearthed or opened until a much later date by people of another time, another era, another experience. The hope is that when people of some future era uncover the time capsule and examine the objects placed within, the experience of the past will come alive for them. By looking over the objects of the time capsule and seeking explanations of those items that are foreign and mysterious, the people who unearth the time capsule will come to enter into the experience of the people who buried it years before. In doing so, a connection is made between the past and the present. The Bible attempts to do the very same thing for us. Not only is the Bible God's Library, it is also the time capsule of the people of Israel and the early Church.

My, How Things Have Changed!

Change used to occur very slowly in our world—until the Industrial Revolution, that is. Cultures and societies that remained virtually unchanged for century after century suddenly faced an explosion of inventions that changed the face of the world forever. Today, change is occurring at such a rapid rate that it is quite reasonable to assume that something that was brand new only a few years ago is now completely obsolete. No doubt, the computer on which I typed this book is by now considered a dinosaur.

Think of all of the things that just a few short years ago were familiar household items that today are completely foreign to many young people. Here's a sampling:

• 45 rpm records

• Beta VCRs

• 8-track tapes

• mimeograph machines

• filmstrips

• phones with dials

• flashcubes

• dot matrix printers

• typewriters

• slide rules

• 8 mm movie film

The list could go on. The point is, in just a few short years, things can change so much that we can lose any knowledge or understanding of how things used to work.

Now, think of the Bible. We're no longer talking about a few short years or even a few short decades or even a few short centuries (or even a few short millennia). Much of the Bible was written over two thousand years ago. If you think things have changed a great deal over the past few years, imagine how much has changed over the last two or three thousand years. Not to mention the fact that the Bible comes to us from a land several thousand miles away from where most of us live and was written in a language quite different from the one spoken in your town square or around the water fountains of your office. It is no wonder that some of the following items taken from the Bible might seem as strange to us as an 8-track tape or a mimeograph machine might seem to our young people:

an ephah	a cubit	manna
fig trees	shekel	centurions
myrrh	pharaoh	lyre
diadem	drachma	dromedary
scroll	mammon	sackcloth

Those are just things. What about names and places?

Sadducees	Ephesus	Esau
Capernaum	Meribah	Pharisees
Zealots	Jairus	Lake Gennesaret
Boaz	Nicodemus	Sanhedrin

It's no wonder that we sometimes get a little frustrated when we read the Bible and come across some of these names of things, people, or places that may mean absolutely *nothing* to us. It is as though we are looking through someone else's photo album without them present to explain what and who we are looking at. Without some assistance, we will find ourselves scratching our heads and concluding that the Bible must have been written for scholars and not for us. Fortunately, help is right at our fingertips. In fact, God's Library has help built right in. The Bible may seem to us like a time capsule that is difficult to understand in our contemporary times, but the secrets of the past can be revealed to us by reading the tiny little print at the bottom of each Bible page. Prepare to enter the world of footnotes, cross-references, concordances, and commentaries. Before we do that, however, try testing your biblical knowledge of some of the items mentioned in the previous list.

A Multiple Choice Quiz

Explanations and definitions of the following items can be found in Bible footnotes. Test your knowledge of these Bible people, places, things, etc.

1. *Ephah* refers to: a) the place where the Ephesians lived b) a unit of measure equal to one yard c) a dry measure equal to half a bushel d) the place where Moses received the ten commandments

2. *Manna* refers to: a) the Hebrew word for Man b) the substance the Israelites ate in the desert c) the town where Zacchaeus lived d) a reference to money or material things

3. A *Drachma* is: a) another name for a camel b) an ancient Greek silver coin c) property a bride brings to a marriage d) a turban-like crown

4. *Lyre* refers to: a) a stringed instrument similar to a harp b) a small town in Judea c) a form of Roman currency d) the name of an Old Testament woman

5. A *Scroll* is: a) the name given to a Jewish priest b) a Greek word meaning "synagogue" c) a unit of measure equal to a foot d) a book formed out of rolled up papyrus

6. *Esau* refers to: a) the village where Jesus raised Lazarus from the dead b) the name of a temple official c) the name of Jacob's brother d) the name of one of the 12 apostles

7. *Jairus* is the name of: a) the man whose daughter Jesus raised from the dead b) the tax collector Jesus called down from the tree c) the town toward which 2 disciples walked when Jesus appeared to them d) the father-in-law of Moses

8. The *Sadducees* were: a) a fourth-century B.C. Egyptian dynasty b) people who were very sad, you see? c) a separatist sect living in the desert d) a priestly aristocracy from which came the high priest

9. *Nicodemus* was: a) a member of the Sanhedrin who came to Jesus at night b) one of the criminals crucified next to Jesus c) the high priest who sent Jesus to Pilate d) the name of the first Gentile converted by Paul

10. *Ephesus* is the name of: a) the town whose walls fell down at the trumpet's blast b) Peter in Greek c) the city to which Paul addressed his letter to the Ephesians d) one of the twelve tribes of Israel

Answer Key: 1.c 2.b 3.b 4.a 5.d 6.c 7.a 8.d 9.a 10.c

Footnotes, Cross-references, Concordances, and Commentaries to the Rescue

Here's a Bible passage from the book of Deuteronomy concerning a law of marriage that at first glance may seem difficult to understand. Read it over and see how much of it makes sense to you.

5 When brothers live together and one of them dies without a son, the widow of the deceased shall not marry anyone outside the family; but her husband's brother shall go to her and perform the duty of a brother-in-law by marrying her. 6 The first-born son she bears shall continue the line of the deceased

brother, that his name may not be blotted out from Israel. 7 If, however, a man does not care to marry his brother's wife, she shall go up to the elders at the gate and declare, "My brother-in-law does not intend to perform his duty toward me and refuses to perpetuate his brother's name in Israel." 8 Thereupon, the elders of his city shall summon him and admonish him. If he persists in saying, "I am not willing to marry her," 9* his sister-in-law, in the presence of the elders, shall go up to him and strip his sandal from his foot and spit in his face, saying publicly, "This is how one should be treated who will not build up his brother's family." 10 And his lineage shall be spoken of in Israel as "the family of the man stripped of his sandal." (Dt 25:5–10)

The idea of spitting in someone's face is easily understood and even today would be seen as a humiliating gesture. But, what's all this about stripping a man of his sandal? It seems far worse to have someone spit in your face than to take away a shoe. Yet, this passage tells us that the people of Israel will remember the ne'er-do-well brother-in-law, *not* as the one who had his face spat upon, but as the "man *stripped of his sandal.*" What's going on here? How do we understand this passage? What does it mean to us today? Where do we go for help?

The answer may lie at the bottom of the page in your Bible on which this passage is located (depending on which Bible translation you're using). You'll notice that in this translation, verse 9 has an asterisk next to it. This is an indication of a footnote concerning this verse. Different Bibles use different symbols to indicate a footnote: an asterisk, a cross, consecutive letters of the alphabet, or some other symbol. In any case, a symbol like the asterisk you see for verse 9 is telling the reader that there's an explanation waiting for you in the footnote section of that page. Like an archeologist and a theologian standing on either side of you to explain something you've unearthed from an ancient time capsule, the footnote provides an explanation of a confusing or curious passage. For example, the footnote for verse 9 in the New American Bible reads like this:

> 25:9 The penalty decreed for a man who refuses to comply with this law of family loyalty is public disgrace (the widow is to spit in his face) and the curse of poverty; sandals were proverbially a man's cheapest possession (cf Am 2, 6; 8,6), and therefore "a man without sandals" was the poorest of the poor.

Aha. Now, we are getting somewhere. Here's an example of a phrase that meant one thing to certain people a few thousand years ago and holds little meaning for us today. Yet, when we read the footnote provided in God's Library, we see clearly how this act of removing a man's sandal was understood as a symbol of disgrace and a curse. Further, this footnote gives a cross-reference to the book of Amos. The letters *cf* (see also) in the footnote indicate another passage that we should look up. If we find Amos 2:6 we discover the following quote:

> Thus says the Lord: For three crimes of Israel, and for four, I will not revoke my word; Because they sell the just man for silver, and the poor man for a pair of sandals.

Likewise, in Amos 8:6 we find this:

> We will buy the lowly man for silver, and the poor man for a pair of sandals.

The footnote and the cross-references provide the reader with a clearer understanding of why this action of stripping a man of his sandal would be seen as such a powerful gesture. With this knowledge, we can go back to the original passage and reread it with a fuller understanding of what it meant to the people of Israel and the role that the Law had in their lives. This may seem like a lot of work, but it is well worth it if we remember that we are reading the story of *our* salvation history. There are other payoffs as well. Once you look up a footnote or a cross-reference, you come away with an understanding that deepens your overall comprehension of the Bible. Chances are if you bump into a confusing word or phrase in one passage, it will come up in another. If you've done your homework and looked up the footnote or a cross-reference, you'll have a better understanding of it the next time it comes around. For example, take a look at the following passage which you've probably read numerous times:

> Now the people were filled with expectation, and all were asking in their hearts whether John might be the Messiah. John answered them all saying, "I am baptizing you with water, but one mightier than I is coming. I am not worthy to loosen the thongs of his sandals." (Lk 3:15–16)

Now that our research has revealed that a man's sandal was his cheapest possession, we see just how profound a statement John the Baptist is making about himself: he declares himself unworthy to even touch Jesus' cheapest possession, namely, his sandal. By the way, we've also answered the age-old complaint of many Christians who feel that reading the Old Testament is a waste of time, thinking that it has nothing to teach us about Jesus. Think again. The Old Testament understanding of a man's sandal as his cheapest possession sheds light on this New Testament passage concerning John the Baptist's perspective on Jesus.

Footnotes provide us with explanations for many things. Here are some examples, just to name a few:

•the meaning(s) of a word, phrase, or custom

•the historical setting of a story

•geographical locations

•important dates

•how certain stories and people are related

•references to other languages and nuances that may be lost in English

•theological insight

•patterns to watch for

•customs and traditions of biblical peoples

•cross-references to similar occurrences of the same word, phrase, person, or situation

Footnotes hold the key to unlocking the secrets of God's Library. Footnotes provide the tool for scraping away centuries of "dirt and mud" to discover the true meaning of a time capsule we call the Word of God. By using footnotes, you will be able to see many passages in the Bible in a whole new light. Footnotes didn't just appear in the Bible. We can thank Scripture scholars and archeologists who have literally and painstakingly dug and scraped until they uncovered insights into the past that allow us to bring the Word of God to the present and carry it into the future. For that reason, it's important to have a Bible that incorporates the best of Catholic Scripture scholarship. We'll talk more about selecting a Bible later. Now, before we take a closer look at the idea of cross-references that may occur without a footnote, let's practice looking up some footnotes.

Practicing Your Footnote Finesse

Read the following Scripture stories while searching all of the footnotes indicated in your Bible. Make a brief list of any new information you learn.

Noah's Ark (Gn 6:5–22)

The Covenant with Abram (Gn 15)

The Call of Moses (Ex 3:4–22)

Psalm 22

The Genealogy of Jesus and the Birth of Jesus (Mt 1)

The Vocation of Saul (Acts 9:1–30)

The Woman and the Dragon (Rev 12)

What Are All Those Numbers?

Footnotes may seem confusing at first glance until we learn how to follow the symbols pointing us to their information. In the same way, *cross-references* may look extremely confusing. We may find a column near the bottom of our Bible page containing an extensive list of numbers and Bible passages. It may look like this:

| † | 6f: | Prv 8:14f |
| | 8: | Prv 1:6; Sir 39:1ff; 42:19f; Dn 2:21 |

10ff: 1Kgs 3:28; Jb 29:8ff, 21f
13:     Sir 15:6; 41:12f; Is 56:5

What's all this, then? Once again, you need to look for symbols that your Bible is using. In our example above, notice that at the top left of the list, you will find the following symbol: † This means that wherever you see this symbol (†) in your text, there is a cross-reference on the page telling you where you can find another passage dealing with the same or related topic, story, character, etc. For example, if you were to read about Jesus' arrest in the gospel of John, you will find at the beginning of Jn 18:1 a symbol indicating that the same story may be found in the following places:

Mt 26:30

Mk 14:26

Lk 22:39

By looking up the cross-references, you can compare how one gospel tells the story in comparison to another. In the same way, a New Testament passage may echo something from the Old Testament. For example, if you read the following passage in Luke chapter four describing Jesus' appearance in the synagogue, notice the indication of a cross-reference:

17 When the book of the prophet Isaiah was handed him, he unrolled the scroll and found the passage where it was written:

18 †"The spirit of the Lord is upon me;
because he has anointed me

to bring glad tidings to the poor.
He has sent me to proclaim liberty to captives and
recovery of sight to the blind,
to let the oppressed go free,
19 and to proclaim a year acceptable to the Lord."

If you are a curious reader, you may ask yourself, "Where can I find that passage in Isaiah?" Enter the cross-reference. At the beginning of the Isaiah quote (verse 18), you see the symbol (†) telling you to look at the cross-reference section of the page. In the cross-reference section, you look for the chapter and verse you are reading, namely Lk 4:18. There, you will find the following:

18: Is 61:1f

Now that you know how to read Scripture citations properly and you can use your abbreviation index in the table of contents, you know that you are looking for *Isaiah, chapter sixty-one, verse one* (the *f* indicates the following verse is also included; *ff* indicates the following verses). Likewise, if you happen to be reading Is 61:1 and think to yourself, "This sounds familiar. Didn't Jesus say these words?" the cross-reference on Is 61:1 will direct you to look at Lk 4:18. Isn't *that* convenient?

Recall our earlier discussion about how different Bibles abbreviate books differently? The same caution needs to be made here about cross-references and footnotes. Different translations or editions of the Bible may have a different approach to cross-references. Some editions will list cross-references in the column directly next to the text. Others will simply list cross-references at the bottom of the page without using any symbols or asterisks. Still others may not even use cross-references at all. By the same token, foot-notes are approached in a variety of styles depending on the Bible translation you are using. Some footnote extensively, others very little. Some use symbols while others use letters. The important thing is to read the introductory pages of your Bible to identify how cross-references and footnotes are used in your Bible.

Cross-references will send you traveling all over the Bible, enabling you to make more connections than the electrical wiring in your house. Once again, by using cross-references (in the same way you benefit from using foot-notes), you will be able to unleash the full power of God's Word by opening doors from one passage to another and from one insight to another. For practice, use your Bible to try locating cross-references to the following gospel stories from Matthew:

The Birth of Jesus (Mt 1:18)

The Baptism of Jesus (Mt 3:13)

The Temptation (Mt 4:1)

The Golden Rule (Mt 8:12)

Jesus Feeds Five Thousand (Mt 14:13)

The Entry into Jerusalem (Mt 21:1)

The Holy Eucharist (Mt 26:26)

The Agony in the Garden (Mt 26:36)

The Women at the Tomb (Mt 28:1)

Next, let's look at what happens when our footnotes and cross-references aren't enough.

The Biblical Concordance

Recall our earlier discussion of *bibliaphobia*. We addressed the fact that one of the reasons many of us are afraid of the Bible is its sheer length. Most Bibles are between one and two thousand pages in length with print so small that it can put a strain on one's eyes. Add to that the dizzying numbers of footnotes and cross-references and each page can become quite involved. Unfortunately, despite all of the information given in the footnotes and cross-references, we have only scratched the surface of possible background information on each Scripture passage. If some kind of footnote or cross-reference were included on every name, every date, every location, etc., in the Bible, it would increase the length of our Bibles from one or two thousand pages to ten or twenty thousand pages. For that reason, only the most essential information is given to us in footnotes and cross-references right in our Bibles. Additional information, however, is available in what we call a biblical concordance (sometimes referred to as a dictionary-concordance). Today, a wide variety of biblical concordances are available not only in book form, but also on CD-ROM, that contain the following:

- literally tens of thousands of subject entries

- nearly a million words that occur in the Bible

- every name in the Bible

- descriptions of biblical places and daily life of the Hebrew people

- summaries of each book of the Bible

- historical background

...and more. At one time, biblical concordances were primarily a tool for Scripture scholars and university study. Today, however, concordances are available and quite useful for the average Christian's personal Bible study and prayer. Just as your grammar school teachers taught you to always read literature with a dictionary at hand, so too a biblical concordance should be nearby when you are reading the Bible. The Bible need not remain a mystery to us. Likewise, it is not necessary for the average Catholic to enroll in college or university theology classes to gain access to biblical information. Scholars have already done that work for us and have placed the fruits of their labor at our fingertips in these very valuable volumes (available at most bookstores). With a concordance at our side, each time we read the Bible it is as though we have a Scripture scholar sitting beside us to answer our every question.

Biblical Commentaries

Finally, even with our numerous footnotes, cross-references, and concordance information, sometimes we still need assistance in understanding the meaning and significance of specific passages within the context of the whole chapter, book, testament, or even the whole Bible. At times like this, we need the assistance of biblical commentaries. Commentaries are basically essays that lead us chapter by chapter and verse by verse through each book of the Bible, providing us with a more detailed and holistic explanation of the Scripture passages we are reading. Commentaries are very helpful for those involved in Scripture study, preaching, pastoral ministry, or catechesis. However, personal prayer can be greatly enhanced as well by reading biblical commentaries. After reading a Scripture passage, it is often

51

helpful to browse through a commentary before returning to the passage and prayerfully rereading it. With the depth and background provided by the commentary, the Word of God comes to life for us in a way that was not previously possible. Using a commentary to enhance our personal Scripture study and prayer is like plugging in an electrical device that previously did not work—the potential was there all along but the connection needed to be made!

Using Your "Archeological" Tools

If we think of the Bible as a time capsule, containing valuable and meaningful treasures buried under centuries of dirt and mud, then we should think of footnotes, cross-references, concordances, and commentaries as the archeological tools we need to scrape away that which prevents us from encountering the full power of God's Word. With these tools at our fingertips, we are now ready to forge ahead and make some startling discoveries about the Bible and how it can make a profound impact on our daily living.

Questions for Reflection and Discussion

•If you were to assemble a time capsule that captured the most significant and essential events, people, fads, news stories, etc., of the past year, what would you include?

•If you assembled such a time capsule, what might people 100 years from now have difficulty recognizing or understanding?

•Name something you have that is now obsolete but was considered "state of the art" only a short time ago.

•What part of the Bible have you had the most difficulty understanding?

•Browse through the Bible and search out a few footnotes. What is something you learned from reading a footnote that you did not know before?

•Do the same with a few cross-references. What is something you learned about a passage by comparing its cross-references?

•In what ways can a biblical concordance enhance your personal study of the Bible?

•How can biblical commentaries be of assistance to you in your understanding of the Bible?

FOUR

Truth or Fact?

So, then, is it true that...

• God created the world in seven days?

• Adam lived to be 930 years old?

• Noah built an ark and got two of *every* animal to board it?

• Jonah was swallowed by a whale?

• The walls of Jericho fell at the blast of a trumpet?

• Samson lost all of his physical strength when he got his hair cut?

• David slew a giant named Goliath with a slingshot?

• Jesus survived forty days and forty nights in the desert without food?

• Tongues of fire appeared over the apostles on the feast of Pentecost?

• Only 144,000 will be saved at the end of the world?

How are we to understand the Bible? We may believe that the events listed above are literal truth and did happen (or will happen) just the way the Bible describes them. Such an approach affirms the awesome and almighty power of God who can accomplish anything God wants. It may also lead one to wonder why such miraculous events no longer occur today in the same manner. Did God act one way in biblical times and another way in contemporary times? On the other hand, we may conclude that these events did not occur just the way the Bible describes them but are "just stories." This conclusion solves the riddle of why God seemingly acted different ways in different times. Unfortunately, this approach may also lead one to conclude that the Bible is simply a collection of fairy tales, to be lumped together with those of Aesop and the Brothers Grimm.

How we answer this question touches the very core of our faith and our understanding of how God communicates with us in life as well as through sacred Scripture. Without any further ado, allow me to propose an answer that captures the essence of the *Catholic* approach to understanding the Bible: Everything in the Bible is *true*...but not necessarily *fact*.

The way this answer is phrased is critical. Let there be no doubt that the Bible communicates the absolute *truth* of God. At the same time, understand that *truth* and *fact* are not the same thing. This answer is not meant to be tricky or gimmicky. It is intended to be a profound response to all those who question whether or not the Bible is God's Word or just a collection of stories. Make no mistake about it, the Bible *is* the Word of God and everything in it is true. Equally as important, this answer is offered as a more authentic, orthodox, and effective reply than the unfortunate and damaging reply of, "No, these things didn't really happen...they're just stories." Too many well-intentioned pastors, teachers, catechists, and pastoral ministers have used this reckless reply in their attempts to provide their students with a more mature and contemporary approach to the Bible. Instead of leading people to a deeper understanding of the Bible, the "they're just stories" approach minimizes the power of God's Word, leading people to abandon the Bible. Finally, the caveat included in the statement above (...but not necessarily *fact*) is directed at those who might espouse a *fundamentalist* (literal) approach to the Bible that leads people to a narrow-minded approach to God's Word. While a literal approach to the Bible expands the power of God in biblical stories, it creates a chasm between those stories and our own contemporary personal experience (i.e., God used to appear in burning bushes but doesn't anymore), thus minimizing the power of God in our everyday life. When we say that everything in the Bible is *true*, but not necessarily *fact*, we do not diminish the power of God either in the Bible or in our experience. Likewise, we do not diminish the importance of the Bible but instead raise it up to a new height of importance, challenging readers and believers to approach it in a manner that no other literature is approached. God's Library is no ordinary library and its contents cannot be understood in the same way that other books are understood.

Understanding Myth in a Literal Society

In order to truly understand the Bible, we need to go back and understand the culture in which it was written; a culture that understood *stories* and the concept of *myth* in a much different way from how we tend to understand them today. We live in a very literal culture. Through the knowledge of science, we have the power to prove almost anything. If something cannot be proven, it is considered false. Today, when we refer to something as a story, we are suggesting that what is being communicated is not true. Likewise, our use of the word *myth* carries very negative connotations.

When someone concocts a tall tale, we call it a "myth." As a result, the word myth is almost synonymous with the word lie or falsehood.

Not so in biblical culture.

The difference between contemporary culture and cultures of biblical times can be traced to an understanding of the difference between truth and fact. In the cultures of biblical times, stories and myth were seen as the vehicles by which the most essential and sacred truths of a people were communicated and passed on. That which a people most believed in and considered most sacred was captured in the form of story and myth so that each generation could come to know the essential truths of life. Scientific proof was not available, nor was it needed in order to pass on what the heart held as absolute and essential. Today, unless something is substantiated by facts, we consider it false. In biblical times, truth could be conveyed whether or not the facts were all straight. Since the society did not base its sense of truth on literal interpretation, facts were of secondary importance. In other words, biblical cultures understood that something can be *true* but need not be a *fact*. At first, this may sound outrageous. However, a closer look at our own culture and use of language reveals that we still allow this phenomenon to occur quite regularly in everyday speaking. Read the following paragraph and pay attention to the phrases in italics.

> My kids were *driving me up the wall*. Here I am trying to get to church on time and these little *rugrats* are *tearing up the place*. I'm *pulling my hair out* to keep some kind of order in the house and they don't *give a hoot*. *They kill me*. *To top it all off*, when I leave the

house, it's *raining cats and dogs*. Since I left my umbrel-
la at work, *I'm up the creek without a paddle*. So I have
to *hotfoot* it to the car while *juggling* these two kids.
Naturally, we *drowned*. Then, when we get to within a
block of church, this train with a *billion* cars going
about *one mile per century* is *crawling* along. I *blew my
top*. After waiting there about *three days*, we finally got
to church and sat down just as Father was giving a talk
about getting to church on time. *I just about died.*

What you've just read is a true story. The events
described truly occurred. However, many of the phrases
used to describe these events are not at all factual. As long
as you understand the use of figurative language, you have
no problem accepting the story as true. You would never
pause to ask, "Is is true that cats and dogs were falling from
the sky?" The use of the phrase *cats and dogs* conveys truth
without using fact. As long as you understand figurative language, the recklessness of the facts doesn't faze you. It is
this understanding of figurative language that allows us to
conclude that everything in the Bible is *true*, but not everything in the Bible is a *fact*. With this in mind, let's take a
closer look at some examples from Scripture.

•**Is it true that Adam lived to be 930 years old?** If you understand that the biblical authors use age in the Hebrew
Scriptures to make a point, you'll get it. In Jewish culture (as
in many others), to live a long life is considered to be a
blessing from God. Adam, who was the father of all, was
truly blessed ·and his age represents that. As the stories in
Genesis continue on, the ages begin to decrease as the sinfulness of humankind escalates. The use of age here is not
intended to represent fact but to convey truth: God's bless-

ing is gradually being rejected by humankind who are in need of salvation.

• **Is it true that Noah built an ark and got two of every species of animal on board to survive a flood that washed out all of humankind?** The fact is, there may very well have been a flood and an ark. We don't know. Consider this: in today's world, because of mass communication and technology, our world has been transformed into a global village. When something happens on one side of the world, the rest of the world can watch it on the news. In primitive cultures, this was not true. The world's boundaries were limited by the limited knowledge of geography. A devastating flood could easily have wiped out the "world" as it was known at the time by a particular culture. Such tragedies were always seen as punishment from God. Perhaps a just man named Noah did survive with his family and his farm animals. The simple matter is, we don't know the facts. However, we do know that this is a true story. The story teaches us the sacred and essential truth that humankind will drown in sinfulness. The only thing that will keep one afloat is to live an upright life. Sinfulness is punished and goodness is saved. God replenishes that which God has created. Someday, perhaps someone will find Noah's ark and prove that the story is indeed factual. In the meantime, we already know that it's a true story.

• **Is it true that the Garden of Eden exists?** In the book of Genesis, we are told that the Garden of Eden exists where four rivers meet: the Pishon, the Gihon, the Tigris, and the Euphrates. All you need to do is to discover where these four rivers meet and you'll have discovered the Garden of Eden. The only problem is, these four rivers do not meet. Is the Bible lying to us? Is the Bible false? No. These four rivers *do* meet...in the land of myth. The biblical author is alerting us to the fact that the following story is *sacred*. The reader is being forewarned: prepare to enter into sacred space and confront an essential truth of life. These four rivers do not factually meet. Yet this is a true story.

•**Is it true that God created the world in seven days?** If we believe the creation story literally, what do we do about the theories of the "big bang" and evolution? If we believe the big bang theory and the theory of evolution, does that make the Bible's version false? No. We don't have to take sides. The Bible story of creation in seven days is a true story. Likewise, the second story of creation found in Genesis chapter two is *also* true. The Bible itself doesn't give us only one account of creation but instead gives us two stories—which one is true? They *both* are. Even though the *facts* of the two stories conflict, they both teach us certain sacred and essential truths: creation comes from God; all of creation is good and blessed; man and woman are made in the image of God; humankind is responsible for caring for creation; and the idea of resting once per week is divine. As for the facts concerning the actual process of creation, we don't know. We weren't there when it happened. However, the biblical stories of creation and the theories of the big bang and evolution are not mutually exclusive. As one bumper-sticker puts it: "The Big Bang Theory: God said BANG! and it happened."

•**Is it true that Jonah was swallowed by a whale?** Like every story in the Bible, we need to remind ourselves that the story is not just about a character who lived long ago and far away, it is our story. Every Bible story is somehow the story of your life and my life. The story of Jonah is not a story about whether a man can factually survive in the belly of a whale for three days, but a story about what happens when you and I try to run away from God's call and God's will. Jonah was called by God to preach to the people of Nineveh and call them to repentance. He simply didn't want to do that. So, in the great tradition of Adam and Eve, he tried to run and hide. This story teaches us the very sacred and essential truth of life: you can run but you can't hide from God. Jonah boards a ship, is blamed for causing a storm to erupt because he disobeyed his God, and is tossed overboard only to be swallowed by a whale. It is in the belly of the whale that conversion happens to Jonah. After three days and three nights (pay attention to the use of numbers—more on that will be coming up soon), Jonah has a change of heart and proceeds to call the people of Nineveh to repentance. This true story teaches us that when we run from God, we encounter storms, darkness, and isolation, and that in our isolation, God can and will find us. God does not give up easily.

• **Is it true that Jesus went forty days and forty nights in the desert without eating any food?** Jesus is the Son of God and can perform miracles beyond explanation. At the same time, he is fully human. No human can survive a month and ten days in the desert without some kind of food. Yet, this is a true story. We mentioned a few moments ago that it's important to pay attention to the use of numbers in the Bible. Here again, we see the use of forty days and forty nights (where have you seen this number used before?). The number forty is highly symbolic. It communicates a "significant period of time." Recall that the people of Israel passed through the waters of the Red Sea and spent forty years wandering through the desert, often tempted because of lack of food. Jesus now has passed through the waters of his baptism and is led into the desert where he too is tempted. Israel failed her test. Jesus is triumphant. Is it a fact that Jesus spent a month and ten days in the barren desert without eating any food? We don't know. But the truth is that for a significant period of time, parallel to the time Israel spent in the desert, Jesus faced temptation over the question of where nourishment comes from. He concludes that it is not from bread alone but from every word that comes from the mouth of God. We too have crossed through the waters of baptism and endure significant periods of dryness during which we grapple with the question of where our nourishment will come from. Jesus' experience provides us with the answer.

• **Was is light or was it dark?** The gospel of Mark tells us that the women came to the tomb on the that first Easter morning, "very early when the sun had risen" (Mk 16:2). The gospel of John tells us that they came upon the tomb, "while it was still dark" (Jn 20:1). This conflict may cause us trouble if we are looking for the literal time of the resurrection. When did they come to the tomb? If the sun had risen, it would be bright and not still dark. Which story is true? They both are. The gospel of John uses the images of light and dark throughout: "the light shines in the darkness" (1:5), "whoever lives the truth comes to the light" (3:21), "I am the light of the world" (9:5), "I came into the world as light" (12:46). It makes sense to have the women arrive at the tomb "while it was still dark," to reinforce the image that the people who "walk in darkness" will soon see "a great light" (also reminiscent of Isaiah 9:2). The fact that these two stories describe the same event, yet use different "facts" reinforces the notion that the authors are not as concerned with literal facts, as we are today, but are instead concerned with communicating the truth: namely, that Jesus, the light of the world, is risen.

• **Was it on the mount or on the plain?** We are all familiar with Jesus' famous discourse referred to as the "Beatitudes" (i.e. Blessed are the poor in spirit...). Interestingly enough, Matthew's gospel tells us that Jesus delivered this sermon on "the "mountain" (mount) while Luke's gospel tells us that it was delivered on "level ground" (plain). Simply put, a mount is not a plain. Which story is true? Once again, *both.* The authors are not concerned with the fact of where Jesus stood but instead with the truth of his teaching. Matthew's gospel is written to an audience that was predominantly Jewish. A Jewish audience would need a great deal of convincing to believe that Jesus was a greater prophet than Moses. What better way to do this than to have Jesus deliver his new "commandments" from atop a mountain, just as Moses received the Ten Commandments on Mount Sinai? The facts of where Jesus actually stood are overpowered by the truth being communicated here: Jesus is a prophet far greater even than Moses.

References to Numbers and Locations
As you read the Bible, pay close attention to the use of numbers and locations. References to such "facts" are often a clue to some deeper symbolic meaning. While anthropology has substantiated numerous historical, geographical, and numerical references in the Bible, quite often the authors were not as interested in the facts as we tend to be, but were instead using numbers and locations as a tool for communicating something symbolic. Let's take a closer look at each of these.

Numbers: The Bible loves to use numbers. Some numbers are good. Some are bad. Some numbers are repeated so often that we can rightly become a bit suspicious and ask, "what's going on here?" We've already talked a little bit about the number forty. How often do we see this? Well, guess what the answer to all of the following questions is:

• How many days and nights did it rain for Noah?

• How many days did it take to embalm Jacob?

• How many years old were both Jacob and Esau when they got married?

• How many years did the Israelites wander through the desert?

• How many years did both David and Solomon rule as king?

• How many years old was Moses when he slew an Egyptian?

• How many years later did Moses encounter the burning bush?

• How many days was Moses on the mountaintop before he came down with the commandments?

• How many days did it take Moses' scouts to reconnoiter the land of Canaan?

• How many days and nights did Goliath take his stand before meeting up with David?

• How many days and nights did Elijah walk strengthened by the food and drink he received?

• How many days' warning did Jonah give the people of Nineveh?

•How many days and nights did Jesus spend in the desert without food?

•How many days did Jesus remain with his disciples after the resurrection?

The answer to *all* of the above: *forty*. In fact, the number forty occurs over 80 times in the Bible. This is a clue that it is being used as a symbol and not strictly to communicate fact. Deuteronomy 8:2 tells us about the significance of the number forty:

> Remember how for forty years now the Lord your God has directed all your journeying in the desert, so as to test you by affliction and find out whether or not it was your intention to keep his commandments.

In other words, the number forty represents a significant period of time during which a person's faithfulness is tested and can be judged or determined. Other numbers are used frequently in the Bible to convey symbolic meaning. Here are a few more samples:

•The number three (3) appears hundreds of times in the Bible. In biblical tradition, it is always on the third day that God saves. The angel intervened to stop Abraham from sacrificing Isaac on the third day. After three days in the desert without water, God provided fresh water through Moses. The prophet Hosea says, "He will revive us after two days: on the third day he will raise us up to live in his presence." (Hos 6:2). Jonah emerged from the whale on the third day. Paul regained his sight on the third day. Mary and Joseph found the twelve-year-old Jesus in the temple on the third day. Jesus fed 4000 people after they had been with him for three days with nothing to eat. Jesus rose from the dead on the third day. The book of Exodus gives us a clue about the significance of the third day when it says, "'Go to the people...make them wash their garments and be ready for the third day; for on the third day the Lord will come down on Mount Sinai before the eyes of all the people.' ...On the morning of the third day there were peals of thunder and lightning and a heavy cloud over the mountain, and a very loud trumpet blast, so that all the people in the camp trembled...for the Lord came down upon it in fire" (Ex 19:10–11,16,18). Needless to say, the number three is one of those "good" numbers in the Bible because God always comes through on the third day.

•The number six (6), on the other hand, is not such a good number. Not that it's bad, but it tends to represent incompleteness. Noah was 600 years old when the flood came. Pharaoh sent 600 first-class chariots to chase after the Israelites. God worked for six days to create the heavens and the earth but blessed and made holy the seventh day for rest. Of course, in the book of Revelation, the "beast" is represented by the number 666. Think about that: three is a good number, representing completeness. Six represents *in*completeness. 666 or three sixes simply represents complete incompleteness! In other words, the use of 666 in the book of Revelation is not some secret code to tell us who the anti-Christ will be. It is simply a symbolic way of representing evil in whatever form it may take in any age.

•The number seven (7)...ah, back to the good numbers. Seven tends to represent fullness or perfection. God rested on the seventh day. Noah took seven pairs of all clean animals aboard the ark. The walls of Jericho came crumbling down after seven days of trumpet playing. Jesus tells Peter to forgive his brother seventy times seven times. The book of Revelation speaks to the seven churches. The same book also tells us that the seventh trumpet will signal the end of the world. Whenever we encounter the number seven, it tends to be satisfying.

•Last but not least is the number twelve (12). Twelve, of course, symbolizes first and foremost the fullness of the people of Israel: twelve tribes. The people of Israel discovered an oasis at Elim with twelve streams of water. Jesus, of course, had twelve apostles. And, once again, the book of Revelation tops it all off by telling us that 144,000 people will be saved at the end of the world; a number that is of course, divisible by twelve, representing twelve thousand from each of the twelve tribes of Israel. With this much use of the number twelve, we can be sure that we are dealing with metaphorical language and not facts. In other words, we don't know how many people will be saved at the end of the world, but the truth is: it will symbolize that the people of God have finally reached fullness of life.

The bottom line to all this is that numbers are a clue to the reader: pay attention and look for the deeper meaning. Look for the truth being communicated.

Locations: Many biblical references to locations have proven to be historically accurate. Archeologists have unearthed cities referred to in the Old Testament that were thought to be fictional or at least long gone. Many locations referred to still exist, some in a relatively unchanged state. On the other hand, we encounter many other references to locations that prove troublesome. We've already discussed the problem of the location of the Garden of Eden and the question of whether Jesus delivered the Beatitudes on a mount or on a plain. More questions may arise as we read along: was Jesus really born in Bethlehem? Did the Holy Family really hide away in Egypt? Did Jesus travel to Jerusalem once, as Matthew, Mark, and Luke tell us, or three times as John indicates (notice the use of the number three here)? Why were the two disciples on the road to a place called *Emmaus* after Jesus' death?

The key here is to once again recall our discussion of the difference between truth and fact. The biblical authors were concerned with teaching truth. They were not historians or geographers, and their use of locations is often as symbolic as their use of numbers. Locations conjure up images. Even today, when someone names a location, people can have a reaction, either positive or negative depending on what that location suggests. What are we to learn from these references to location? Often, the footnotes and commentaries will have something to say about these. In the meantime, here are a few clues about some that we just mentioned:

• **Bethlehem:** The prophet Micah refers to Bethlehem saying, "And you, Bethlehem, land of Judah, are by no means least among the princes of Judah, since from you shall come a ruler who is to shepherd my people Israel" (Mi 5:2). It is quite possible that Jesus was historically born in Bethlehem. Whether or not that's a fact of history, the truth is that Jesus is the ruler who came from humble beginnings to become the shepherd of all Israel.

• **Egypt:** The gospel of Matthew is the only gospel that recounts the flight into Egypt. Recall that Matthew was writing to a predominantly Jewish audience familiar with the story of the Exodus. To such an audience, this reference would immediately conjure up images of the time that God called forth his people out of the land of Egypt. In the same way, Jesus would now be seen as called by God out of the land of Egypt to form a new people. We have no proof that Jesus, Mary, and Joseph traveled to Egypt. It is certainly possible. This story teaches us that it is true: Jesus is he who is called to lead the new Israel. (That would be us!)

•**Jesus' travels to Jerusalem:** Matthew, Mark, and Luke tell us that Jesus "cleansed" the temple during his last days as part of his one single journey to Jerusalem. John places this event near the beginning of his ministry and has Jesus returning to Jerusalem a total of three times. We don't know the facts. The truth is, however, that Jerusalem and the temple were seen as the center of Jewish life. John's gospel was written *after* the destruction of the temple in 70 A.D. Such an event would be fresh in the minds of Jewish Christians to whom John was writing. Furthermore, these Jewish Christians were experiencing the turmoil of being "thrown out" of their synagogues as the split between Jews and Jewish Christians deepened and grew acrimonious. John's chronology of Jesus' three visits to Jerusalem and his references to the cleansing of the temple at the beginning of Jesus' ministry may very well be fact. We simply don't know. We do know the truth, however, which is that Jesus is the new center of God's presence in the world, replacing the temple and Jerusalem. And, since God saves on the third day, it makes sense that Jesus' saving action would occur on his third visit to Jerusalem.

•**Emmaus:** Where the heck is Emmaus? Why are two disciples headed there after Jesus' tragic death? Why does the author even tell us this location? The fact is, very little is known about Emmaus. It seems to have absolutely no significance—that's the point. After Jesus' death, the disciples were lost and directionless. The only important thing about Emmaus is that it is headed *away* from Jerusalem. The disciples are attempting to leave behind the experience of Jesus' death. They don't know where they are headed as long as it is away from the past. After their encounter with the Risen Jesus on the road to Emmaus, their destination changes: they make a 180-degree turn and head back to Jerusalem, back to where Jesus' death occurred. Was there really a place called Emmaus? Were two disciples really headed there? We cannot be sure...we have no proof. But we do know the truth: when we are lost and without direction, we do not recognize the presence of the risen Lord in our midst. When we *do* encounter him in the sharing of the Word and the breaking of the bread, *our* eyes are opened, and we can revisit the place of our pain with a new faith.

Personally, my favorite "location" reference is a little known one found in the sixth chapter of Mark's gospel. The chapter begins with Jesus and his disciples in Nazareth. Jesus encounters some difficulty in his own town. He proceeds to send out the twelve. After they come back reporting their success, Jesus invites them to an out of the way place, a deserted region not far from the shore of the Sea of Galilee. In this deserted place, Jesus feeds 5000 people despite the apostles' reluctance. All of this is taking place on the western shore of the Sea of Galilee: Jewish territory. After this incident, Jesus tells the apostles to get in the boat and precede him to the other side of the lake toward Bethsaida: Gentile territory. That evening, the apostles do so, but encounter their own turbulence as they try to row with the wind against them. Between 3 and 6 in the morning (note: they've been rowing since evening...a total of between 9 and 12 hours), Jesus comes walking on the water toward them. After he gets in the boat and the winds calm down, the story tells us the following: *"After making the crossing, they came to land at Gennesaret"* (Mk 6:53). Interestingly enough, Gennesaret is on the *same side of the Sea of Galilee* that they were on *before* they left! After struggling all night rowing against the wind for 9 to 12 hours, they ended up just about where they were before they embarked.

We tend to miss all of this symbolism since we are not familiar with the area. However, audiences familiar with the region would certainly catch the irony in these references to location. Is the author trying to give us historical information about location? Perhaps. But more important, the author is using references to location in order to communicate some very important truths: the twelve apostles (the "church") had a difficult time carrying the gospel across the lake to unfamiliar territory. They could make no headway in the face of turbulence. Only Jesus can rise above this (walking on the water). Jesus alone leads them on to Tyre and Sidon and the district of the Ten Cities, all Gentile areas where, interestingly enough, in chapter 8 of Mark's gospel, he again feeds a huge crowd, this time 4000 people, after they had been with him three days (on the *third day*...). All of these references to location reinforce the powerful messages in these stories...all of which are true.

"But I Need to Have Proof."

Once, when I was delivering a "God's Library" workshop to a group of outstanding young adults in a Chicago suburb, I covered the above examples of figurative language in the Bible and the difference between truth and fact. While the participants listened intently and accepted the approach I was taking, two main concerns surfaced. One was, "if the Bible is not all fact and uses figurative language and stories, that opens the door for anyone to interpret them any way they so desire." The fact is, we are called upon to interpret the Bible in light of our experience. However, we do so within a broader tradition of interpretation that goes back over 2000 years. We are not free to interpret the Bible any old way we please; we do so within the context of our Catholic Christian tradition. It is also important to remember that while the Bible speaks to us personally it does not speak to us exclusively. Our interpretation of the Bible must be done in communion with our present-day brothers and sisters in the church as well as with those who have gone before us marked with the sign of faith.

The second concern the participants raised was even more pointed. One participant applied all of this discussion of figurative language to the story of the resurrection and said, "I understand how this might apply to Noah's ark or some other ancient story, but I have to know that Jesus literally rose from the dead. I need proof of that." I responded that without a doubt, I believe that Jesus is risen. However, I can offer no proof. No one can. Not even the Bible offers conclusive proof. We simply have the astonishing accounts of those who claim their lives were completely transformed by an encounter with the one they recognized as the Risen Jesus. Their stories are overwhelmingly compelling—compelling enough to change the lives of millions of people over the last 2000 years. The resurrection is something we believe in based on faith, not proof. Each time we celebrate the Eucharist, we say, "Let us proclaim the *mystery* of our faith: Christ has died, Christ is risen, Christ will come again!" Ultimately, the Bible does not provide us with proof of anything. It provides us with the compelling testimony of those who have encountered the mystery of faith and invite us to enter into it and experience it more fully. In his book, *Reconstructing Catholicism: For a New Generation* (New York: Crossroad Publishing Company, 1995), Dr. Robert Ludwig captures the flavor of a solid Catholic approach to Scripture when he describes the Bible (the gospels in particular) in the following way:

> It is our story, it is the story of all the earth, a universal story about gracious mystery as our source and destiny and the need to live by courage and trust. Yet, this story is not an "answer" to our questions, as the fundamentalists would have it. Rather, the Gospel is the thematization of our experience of mystery, helping us make peace with our deepest questions by our acceptance of incompleteness, vulnerability, emptiness. (pg. 97)

Finally, it is important here to lend credibility to this whole discussion about the difference between truth and fact. In other words, this is not something I made up. Rather, it is the official position of the Catholic Church as summarized by the Pontifical Biblical Commission's document entitled, "The Interpretation of the Bible in the Church." Here are a few quotations from that document that serve as the foundation for this chapter (all quotes are from *Origins*, January 6, 1994, Vol 23: No. 29):

> •Fundamentalism places undue stress upon the inerrancy of certain details in the biblical texts, especially in what concerns historical events or supposed-

ly scientific truth. It often historicizes material which from the start never claimed to be historical. It considers historical everything that is reported or recounted with verbs in the past tense, failing to take the necessary account of the possibility of symbolic or figurative meaning.

•It is not sufficient to translate a text word for word in order to obtain its literal sense. One must understand the text according to the literary conventions of the time. When a text is metaphorical, its literal sense is not that which flows immediately from a word-to-word translation (e.g. "Let your loins be girt": Lk 12:35), but that which corresponds to the metaphorical use of these terms ("Be ready for action"). When it is a question of a story, the literal sense does not necessarily imply belief that the facts recounted actually took place, for a story need not belong to the genre of history but be instead a work of imaginative fiction.

•Fundamentalism refuses to admit that the inspired word of God has been expressed in human language and that this word has been expressed, under divine inspiration, by human authors possessed of limited capacities and resources. For this reason, it tends to treat the biblical text as if it had been dictated word for word by the Spirit. It fails to recognize that the word of God has been formulated in language and expression conditioned by various periods.

•The fundamentalist approach is dangerous, for it is attractive to people who look to the Bible for ready answers to the problems of life. It can deceive these people, offering them interpretations that are pious but illusory, instead of telling them that the Bible does not necessarily contain an immediate answer to each and every problem. Without saying as much in so many words, fundamentalism actually invites people to a kind of intellectual suicide. It injects into life a false certitude, for it unwittingly confuses the divine substance of the biblical message with what are in fact its human limitations.

•Fundamentalism is right to insist on the divine inspiration of the Bible, the inerrancy of the word of God and other biblical truths included in its five fundamental points. But its way of presenting these truths is rooted in an ideology which is not biblical, whatever the proponents of this approach might say. For it demands an unshakable adherence to rigid doctrinal points of view and imposes, as the only source of teaching for Christian life and salvation, a reading of the Bible which rejects all questioning and any kind of critical research.

•It does not follow from this text that we can attribute to a biblical text whatever meaning we like, interpreting it in a wholly subjective way. On the contrary, one must reject as inauthentic every interpretation alien to the meaning expressed by the human authors in their written text.

•In its attachment to the principle "Scripture alone," fundamentalism separates the interpretation of the

Bible from the tradition, which, guided by the Spirit, has authentically developed in union with Scripture in the heart of the community of faith. It presents itself as a form of private interpretation which does not acknowledge that the church is founded on the Bible and draws its life and inspiration from Scripture.

So you see, everything I've said in this chapter is backed up by the full force of the Vatican's Pontifical Biblical Commission.

Now that we've ventured into the topic of interpretation of the Bible, let's delve even further and explore the notion of authentic Catholic interpretation of the Bible as well as some suggestions for making your own personal time with the Bible more meaningful.

Questions for Reflection and Discussion

• In your own words, describe the difference between truth and fact. What are some examples from everyday language?

• A clever Scripture professor once said, "Everything in the Bible is true...and some of it actually happened." What does this mean? How does it compare with the statement we've used (Everything in the Bible is *true*, but not necessarily *fact*)?

• After reading this chapter, how would you respond to someone who asks you a question like: "Did Adam and Eve really exist?" or "Was there really a Noah's ark?"

• After reading this chapter, how would you respond to someone who accuses you of making the Bible sound like a "fairy tale" by all this talk about the difference between truth and fact?

• For a good laugh, rent the video *Airplane* and make a list of all the figurative language that is portrayed literally. Use this as an exercise in illustrating how complex language can be. For children, locate a copy of *Amelia Bedelia* which illustrates the same point of how comical it can be to take something literally that is meant to be understood figuratively.

• How are numbers and locations used for effect in Bible stories? What are some examples?

• What does the Pontifical Biblical Commission teach us about understanding the Bible in "The Interpretation of the Bible in the Church"? How do you feel about the approach to understanding the Bible that this chapter and this document propose? How does it change your understanding of the Bible? How does it help? How does it challenge?

FIVE

Interpreting and Applying the Bible

What Does the Bible *Really* Say?

In the Polish language, there is a word used to express one's delight after a good meal: *Smasznego!* (smoch-NEH-go). At many a family gathering or at a good Polish restaurant, I have heard this phrase uttered while the one uttering proudly patted his/her belly. What does it mean in English? Well, it means *delicious*. Or, perhaps it means, *MMMMM*. Then again, maybe it really means, *That was great*. The problem is, the English language doesn't really have a word that exactly captures the essence of *Smasznego!* In other words, if you ask several different people what *smasznego* means in English, you may get several different answers depending upon one's interpretation. When we go from one language to another, we need to *interpret* what we believe the original language is attempting to say.

What does this have to do with the Bible? Well, first and foremost, the Bible was *not* written in English. When people get nervous about "interpreting" the Bible, they have to realize that every Bible that is not written in the original language of the author IS an interpretation. Most biblical texts were originally written in Hebrew (Old Testament) or Greek

(New Testament). Between the third and fifth centuries, these were translated into Greek and Latin. As centuries progressed, the Bible was translated into dozens of languages. So, when someone gets upset about "contemporary" translations of the Bible, insisting that we use the "original" English text (usually meaning the King James version), they had better be prepared to read either Hebrew or Greek because there is no such thing as the *original English* text.

Every Bible is an interpretation of the original text. Therefore, we need not be afraid of the word *interpretation* when it comes to the Bible. We are called to interpret the Bible within the context of our faith tradition and within the context of the author's original intent, as best we can ascertain that through scholarly research. Let's take a closer look at how we interpret the Bible as a faith community and as an individual within that faith community.

How Do I Choose a Bible?

If different Bibles employ different interpretations, how can one select a Bible that is consistent with a Catholic approach to the Word of God? First, we need to understand the difference between Catholic and Protestant Bibles. While both are the inspired Word of God, it is important to note that our two traditions have different "floor plans" for organizing God's Library. Both the Catholic and Protestant traditions have developed their own final "list" of which books are considered inspired and thus to be included in the Bible. This final official list is referred to as the *canon*. The Catholic canon contains the 73 books we outlined earlier in this book: 46 Old Testament and 27 New Testament. The Protestant canon includes 66 books, eliminating seven Old Testament books: Tobit, Judith, Wisdom, Sirach

(Ecclesiasticus), Baruch, and 1st and 2nd Maccabees. Why the difference?

In the first century after Christ, rabbis in Palestine gathered to form the canon of the Hebrew Scriptures. They selected the 39 books that were written in Hebrew. Around the same time, Greek-speaking Jews in Alexandria established a canon of 46 books for the Hebrew Scriptures (Old Testament) that included the seven books mentioned above, books that were written in Greek. Gentile Christians in Egypt who used Greek continued to include these seven books in the Old Testament. When St. Jerome translated the Bible into Latin in the fifth century, he opted to go with the Hebrew books only. Thus, these seven books continued to be called into question. During the Reformation in the sixteenth century, Protestants established a canon of 39 Old Testament books and referred to the seven in question as the "apocrypha," meaning "hidden" or "secret." Out of this experience came the King James version, which remained as the standard biblical text in English until the twentieth century. Meanwhile, the Catholic Church at the Council of Trent responded by including these seven "apocryphal" books and referring to them as "deutero-canonical," which meant that they were added to the canon at a later time. So, the first thing to know is that there are differences between Catholic and Protestant Bibles in terms of which books are included.

Well into the twentieth century, the only Catholic versions of the Bible were translated from St. Jerome's Latin version of the fifth century. In 1943, Pope Pius XII called for a Catholic translation based on the earliest available manuscripts and the *original* languages. Since that time, several Bibles have been translated by the work of scholars who were predominantly Catholic. One way to determine if a Bible is a Catholic version is to look for what is called an *imprimatur* (im-pri-MAH-tur) near the inside cover of a Bible. The imprimatur, followed by the name of the Roman Catholic authority issuing it, indicates that the translation is acceptable for use by Roman Catholics.

Which translation do we use in church on Sundays? The *Revised New American Bible* (RNAB) is the translation used in our lectionary that we hear proclaimed at Mass in the United States. It makes sense to use this translation in your own studies and prayer since it will be reinforced at Sunday liturgy. A very popular version of the New American Bible is the *Catholic Study Bible* which provides both extensive footnotes and commentary (something we have discussed at length). Another very popular Catholic Bible is the *New Jerusalem Bible* (NJB). The NJB was translated primarily by Catholic scholars in Great Britain. Another version which is more ecumenical in the makeup of its Scripture scholars but still carries an imprimatur is the *New Revised Standard Version* (NRSV). Without attempting to provide an exhaustive guide to selecting Bibles, suffice it to say that if a Bible carries an imprimatur, it is considered acceptable for Catholic readership, in that it represents Catholic tradition and interpretation. Bibles without an imprimatur are not going to harm you but you may encounter discrepancies and conflicts with Catholic thought that might lead to confusion.

Recognizing Different Types of Literature

When you pick up the mail each morning, what do you do? Most likely, you sort it out...some are pieces of junk mail, some are bills, some are personal letters, etc. You can usually identify what type of mail is contained within just by looking at the outside of the envelope. The way you read each piece of mail depends on how you've sorted and identified it. Junk mail gets tossed without hardly a glance, while personal mail may be read over and over (and kept under your pillow at night!). The more mail you get (and the older and wiser you become), the better able you get at identifying what type of mail it is you are about to read. You even learn not to be fooled by the envelopes that tell you you may have just won $10,000,000.

One of the first steps involved in interpreting the Bible is to learn to identify just what type of literature it is that you are reading. Like sorting out the morning mail, you can separate different types of biblical literature into different categories. Just as we do not read all of our mail the same way, we do not read every type of biblical literature in the same manner. The more we read the Bible, the better able we will become at differentiating a parable from a proverb, a genealogy from a discourse, a psalm from a letter, and a prophecy from a legal code.

The key to determining what type of literature you are reading in the Bible is to look at what you're reading within its broader context. The introduction to the book you are reading will often clue you in as to what type of literature you are about to encounter. Likewise, the footnotes we discussed earlier will often reveal secrets about the type of literature under scrutiny. Finally, any Scripture passage must be interpreted in light of its broader context, namely in relation to the preceding and following chapters and verses.

Let's take a look at an example. Suppose we were reading the following passage:

As in all the churches of the holy ones, women should keep silent in the churches for they are not allowed to speak, but should be subordinate, as even the law says. But if they want to learn anything, they should ask their husbands at home. For it is improper for a woman to speak in the church.

(1 Cor 14:34–35)

What are we to make of a passage like this? If we take this passage literally and isolated from its context, we can conclude that women should not be allowed any speaking roles in our celebrations of the Eucharist. Let's take a look at some key questions we must ask any time we are attempting to properly interpret Scripture:

• **What type of literature is this?** If we go back to the title of the book that this passage is taken from, we find that we are reading from the first *letter* of Paul to the Corinthians. This means that we are reading a *letter* written to a specific group of people who lived in Corinth during the first century A.D. We need to understand the general purpose of Paul's letters and the role they played in the early church. When we recognize this literature as a letter, we recognize that we need to get the flavor of the whole letter before we isolate specific verses.

• **What do we know of the author?** In many books of the Bible, we do not know precisely who the author was. In this passage, we are fortunate enough to know that St. Paul is the writer. The more we know about St. Paul's style of writing and his theology, the better able we are to interpret passages from his work. Paul was not afraid to speak his mind and felt very strongly about the need for order in the community.

•**Who was the "target audience" of this work?** Who were the people of Corinth? In order to understand this passage, we need to learn a little bit about the people it was addressed to. Once again, the introduction to the particular book we are reading will usually give us some good background on the audience. In this example, we discover that the church of Corinth had many problems. Paul felt it was his responsibility to address these problems in a straightforward manner to achieve order in the community.

•**What is the overall thrust of the chapter?** of the book? Taken in isolation, we can conclude that this passage compels us to forbid women to speak in church. However, when we look at the overall context of Paul's first letter to the Corinthians, we find that Paul seems to be contradicting some earlier statements he made about the role of women at worship. In chapter 11 verse 5, Paul writes that "any woman who prays or prophesies with her head unveiled brings shame upon her head." Here, Paul clearly is addressing the possibility of women speaking in liturgical leadership roles. When we return to 14:34–35, we find upon close examination that Paul is referring to the notion of women *asking questions* during the liturgy ("If they want to learn anything they should *ask* their husbands at home" [vs. 35]). Paul has already suggested that women may prophesy (11:5). Here, he is talking about keeping order in the assembly. In fact, the overall context of this chapter and the whole book reveals that Paul is trying to establish liturgical order and reconcile differing factions. Taken in context, Paul is not so much speaking about the role of women as he is speaking about liturgical order and ending chaos and confusion that was reigning at Corinthian liturgical assemblies.

•**How do we interpret this passage for today?** It is our responsibility as individuals within a faith tradition to interpret what this passage is saying to us *today*. Paul was speaking to a culture in which the role of women was profoundly different than it is in most cultures and societies today. His comments on women are the result of the culture in which he was writing. Today, we must ask what the proper liturgical roles are when we gather to celebrate Eucharist, what our present-day understanding of the equality and dignity of women is, and how the words of St. Paul can inspire us to celebrate liturgy with proper respect for its rubrics, roles, and order.

Interpretation Tools: Forms of Criticism

It is through the process of interpretation that the Word of God continues to speak to people throughout the ages. The Bible was written in a time of rural life surrounded by images of shepherds, fishermen, kings, and farmers. When the biblical authors recorded their experiences of God's saving presence in their lives, they did not have a society of cellular phones, computers, the internet, and laser technology. For that reason, it is up to us to interpret the Word of God as it applies to our contemporary situation. Despite the new world we live in, the central experiences of life remain unaltered. The Word of God is timeless. We need only to transport it from its original setting and language to our contemporary situation. In order to do this, Scripture scholars offer us some very helpful tools for interpretation called forms of criticism. Let's take a brief look at some.

•**Historical Criticism:** This form of criticism attempts to ascertain as accurately as possible what the author's original intent was. Historical criticism looks closely at what was happening at the time, what the people of the time were experiencing, and who the author was originally writing to/for. Today, archeology plays an important role in helping us learn as much as we can about the place and times of the passage in question. Another aspect of the historical approach is the attempt to determine who the author actually was. We know today that it was common practice in biblical times to credit a literary work to someone who may not have actually taken pen to paper. Today, we consider that fraud. Recall, however, that the Bible was recorded in a time when most people were illiterate. Most forms of literature were passed along orally for decades if not centuries before they were written down. As with any oral tradition, they take on the flavor of those passing the story along. Since we believe that the Bible is the inspired word of God, we are saying that this entire process was inspired by God. In the end, as long as a piece of literature was said to have been from the tradition of an individual, it was deemed proper to add that person's name to the title of the book. In other words, when we say that something is from the gospel of John or the prophet Isaiah, we are saying that this is indeed the message they conveyed as it was passed down orally for a given period before a scribe or school of scribes collected it, sorted it, edited it, recorded it, and credited it to their name. Once again, this does not take away from the validity of the Bible but reveals how God works through a very human process to shape the Word into flesh. The better we understand this whole process, the closer we are able to come to the original intent of the work before we attempt to apply it to our own lives.

• **Textual Criticism:** When discussing Scripture, we will sometimes hear people say, "If we go back to the *original* text..." It sounds good. All we need to do is go back to the original text and see exactly what was written, translate it as closely as possible into English, and we'll know exactly what the text says. There's only one problem. We have *no* original texts. We do not have any of the psalms written in David's own handwriting on parchment. We have none of Paul's letters on the original stationery. All we have are early manuscripts, the earliest known *copies* of all the works of the Bible. When Scripture scholars "go back to the *original* text," then, they are going back to the earliest available copies. Textual criticism attempts to look at these early manuscripts, many of which contain differences on the same passages, and determine what they said in their *original* language so that the best interpretation can be made when translation is attempted.

•**Form Criticism:** We have previously dealt with the issue of asking what type of literature we are reading and how we should approach it. Form criticism attempts to determine precisely what type of literature we are dealing with, how that form of literature was understood in its time, and how we are to understand it today. Scripture scholar Dianne Bergant, CSA, of the Catholic Theological Union, Chicago, uses a wonderful example in her classes to illustrate how different forms of literature are appropriate for different occasions. She refers to the experience of someone's death. We encounter many forms of literature throughout the experience of one's death:

•a death certificate

•a last will and testament

•an obituary

•a eulogy

• stories

• a homily

All of these forms of literature have a unique purpose and a proper place during the experience of saying good-bye to a loved one. Some are legal documents. Some are informal anecdotes. Some are ritual expressions. We know how to sort these out and put them in their proper place and thus, how to interpret them. Form criticism attempts to do the same. It is a way of sorting out what we are reading in the Bible and determining how to best interpret it given its literary form.

• **Source Criticism:** In today's literal and legalistic society, it is not only proper, but required for authors to indicate where they may have gotten an idea from. To use someone else's idea without giving proper credit is called *plagiarism.* In biblical times, this was not the case. It was common practice for one author to use other sources and edit, delete, incorporate, or expand upon them. Source criticism attempts to determine what previous sources an author may have had at his fingertips and how that source may have influenced the piece we are reading. Here's an example that works a little bit like a word problem or a brain teaser: The gospel of Matthew has over 600 verses in it that appear in Mark's gospel (which many scholars believe was written first). The gospel of Luke, also written after Mark, contains over 300 verses of Mark's gospel. It seems clear that Matthew and Luke relied heavily upon Mark's gospel to write their own. Strangely enough, however, Matthew and Luke *both* share 240 verses in common that are *not* from Mark. Matthew and Luke were not written at the same time or in the same place or by the same author. How can they share 240 verses in common that cannot be traced to another earlier known gospel? This mystery suggests to Scripture scholars that both Matthew and Luke had *another* source separate and different from Mark upon which they relied to write their gospels. Unfortunately, we do not know what this source was. Scripture scholars refer to this mysterious source simply as Q, the first letter of the German word *quelle* which means "source." Source criticism, then, attempts to look at the sources available to biblical authors and how they may have influenced the final product that we may be reading.

• **Redaction Criticism:** Take a look at the end of Mark's gospel. Note that it has 4 endings. The story seems to end at Mk 16:8 when the women leave the tomb in great fear and say nothing to anyone. Next, we encounter something called the "longer ending" from Mk 16:9–20 which includes Jesus appearing to the disciples and ascending to heaven. Following this, we encounter something called the "shorter ending" which captures the essence of the longer ending in just a couple of sentences. Finally, we come upon something called the "Freer Logion." This ending attempts to explain why the disciples were so hesitant to believe. If you read your footnotes and commentaries about these passages, you will notice that each of these endings appears on different early manuscripts and appears to be attempts by editors to provide a more "satisfying" ending than Mark originally did in 16:8. Redaction criticism attempts to discover what portions of Scripture may have been altered or affected by later editors and why. These "alterations" should not be viewed suspiciously, nor should they in any way taint our understanding of the validity of the Scripture we are reading. Rather, they provide a window for us into the minds of people who were attempting to do just what we are doing: discovering a way of making God's Word "fit" into our lives. Their interpretation serves to inspire us to interpret the Bible for our own experience.

All of these forms of biblical criticism are not meant to strip the Bible of its power and mystery but open it up to us as though discovering long lost treasures like those lost on the Titanic or buried in a long lost cave. We ourselves may not conduct the actual scholarly studies and criticisms, but we should use the discoveries made by Scripture scholars to open our eyes to the richness of God's Word and enhance our understanding of the Bible, so that we can apply it to our lives today.

Where To Begin: A Recommended Reading List

Now that you've chosen your translation of the Bible and you're equipped with the knowledge and skills needed to read, study, and interpret the Scriptures, you may be wondering one more thing: where do I begin? If the Bible is indeed a library, then perhaps it would be helpful to recommend some starting points. Here's what I recommend as places to begin:

The Old Testament

1. The book of *Exodus:* the Exodus story is the centerpiece of the entire Old Testament...the "defining moment" of the people of Israel. Besides, you can't go wrong with all of the drama and theatrics of burning bushes, deadly plagues, and parting seas.

2. The book of *Psalms:* the Bible is intended to deepen our faith and our prayer life. What better place to begin than with an entire book of prayers? The Psalms will provide you

with easy reading and profound inspiration for every mood and occasion.

3. The book of *Proverbs:* if you are looking for wisdom, this is a good place to start. Reading Proverbs is like sitting down with your grandparents to get all of the profound insights they have collected through their years of experience. Many people begin and/or end their day with a passage from Proverbs.

The New Testament

1. The *Acts of the Apostles:* this is a good place to start because it is the story we can relate to best: the church struggling to preach the gospel after Jesus' ascension into heaven. The acts of the apostles continue today through us.

2. The *Gospel of Mark:* if you want to get into the gospels right away, begin with Mark. Mark's gospel is the shortest and easiest to read. His "just the facts" approach allows you to cover the whole gospel story in just a few hours, something that is highly recommended.

3. The *Letter of Paul to the Philippians:* sit back and imagine that Paul is writing to you personally. This letter is inspirational and contains one of the most powerful and well-known Christian passages: Phil 2:5–11.

Tips for Reading and Praying the Bible

Typically, when you read a book, you just pick it up and jump right in. Reading the Bible is different. In essence, we do not *read* the Bible, we *pray* the Bible. Once you know what passage you are going to read (keep it short; don't try to take on too much), follow these simple steps:

1. Set a prayerful mood of quiet.

2. Pray to the Holy Spirit to open up your mind and heart to the Word of God.

3. Read the passage once slowly. Look over any footnotes and commentary that will assist your understanding of the passage.

4. Go back and read the passage again, this time more slowly and prayerfully.

5. Be quiet. Let the Word of God continue to echo in your heart, mind, and soul.

6. Pray in your own words thanking God for the Word and asking for the grace you need to apply (interpret) it to your life.

This Is My Story.

The refrain to the wonderful Christian hymn "Blessed Assurance" shouts, "This is my story." We should sing this refrain *every* time we pick up the Bible. Certainly, the Bible is full of stories about people who lived several thousand years ago in a land far, far away from most of us. Ultimately, however, these stories are about us. Each Bible story is somehow the story of your life and my life. The reason these Bible stories are considered sacred and inspired is because throughout the ages, they have been seen as the stories that capture and express the experience of salvation for all people for all time.

As we read and pray the Bible, the ultimate act of interpretation is when we ask the question, "How is this *my* story?" Unless we take this step, the Bible will remain something impersonal and remote. When we ask this question, we open up a whole new relationship in our lives. Now, God is no longer just speaking to Moses, Abraham and Sarah, Jeremiah, Jonah, Peter, Zacchaeus, the woman at the well, Martha and Mary, and Paul. When we read the Bible—Paul's letters, Jesus' words to the apostles—we are hearing God speaking to *us*.

How do we make this happen? How do we make the Bible stories our own? We need to follow two simple steps:

1. First and foremost, we must ask what the text is actually saying and to whom it was originally addressed. We cannot apply the Bible to our lives until we understand the lives of the people who are involved in the story.

2. Second, once we have made an effort to understand the original intent of the author and the experience of the original audience, we must ask the simple and basic question, "How is this story about me?"

When we do this, we realize that:

•The Exodus event was not just about the journey of the people of Israel from slavery in Egypt to freedom in the promised land; it is the story of our own personal journey from the slavery of sin to the freedom we find in the place where we encounter God.

•The story of Jonah and the whale is not just about a cowardly man turned prophet; it is the story of what happens to us whenever we try to run from the will of God—we find that God cannot be outrun.

•The stories of Jesus healing the blind, deaf, paralyzed, and unclean are not just tales of wonder from long ago; they are

stories of how Jesus has the power to heal us when we cannot see, when *our* ears are closed, when we are paralyzed
by fear, greed, or anger, and when we are stained by sin.
The song "Amazing Grace" personalizes the experience by
proclaiming, "I once was lost, but now am found…was
blind but now I see."

•The story of Jesus appearing to the two disciples on the
road to Emmaus is no longer just a mysterious story of two
disciples who could not recognize Jesus but becomes the
story of how we seem to be unable to recognize the Risen
Christ in our midst until we listen to his word and break
bread. In fact this story contains a clue as to how we must
insert ourselves into Scripture stories. It seems that only one
of the two disciples in the story is named: Cleopas. The
other disciple remains unnamed. The author of this story
seems to have done this on purpose in order to entice each
one of us to insert ourselves into the story. We are the other
disciple. We are often directionless. We have experienced
pain and loss. We are unable to recognize the presence of
Jesus even though he walks with us. It is through the reading and study of Scripture that we, like the two disciples on
the road to Emmaus, develop a desire to gather around the
table and break bread, the place where our eyes are opened
and we recognize the presence of the Risen Lord in our
midst.

•We could go on. The story of the woman at the well is the
story of how we thirst. The story of the man born blind is
the story of how we need to see with Jesus' eyes. The story
of the raising of Lazarus is the story of how each of us is
dead, wrapped up, and buried and in need of being called
forth to new life. The story of the passion, death, and res-

urrection of Jesus is the story of how we come to be born again only by dying to our old selves. The story of Pentecost is the story of how we are gifted and sent forth by the spirit to proclaim this Good News to others.

Now Is The Acceptable Time!

During one of my God's Library presentations to a group of 35 to 40 Catholic young adults, one participant admitted that she had only recently begun to learn about the Bible by attending Scripture study. She was excited about the new knowledge and nourishment that she was receiving. I asked her if she was attending this Scripture study at a Catholic church or a Protestant church. She turned red and sheepishly admitted that she was attending a Protestant Bible study. Not wanting to discourage her in any way or proliferate any form of anti-Protestant suspicion, I applauded her zeal. I commented that while I would prefer that she attend a Catholic Bible study, if none were being offered, it was good that she was being nourished by the Word of God from our Protestant brothers and sisters. Before I could move on, another participant strongly objected, not out of any distrust of Protestants but out of a sense of shame that no Catholic churches in the area were offering Bible study. He said, "If there are no Bible studies in any of the area Catholic churches, then, by God, we had better start one...now!" During the break, I observed as several participants surrounded the pastor eagerly offering to help set up a Bible study program for the parish. (See the Appendix for suggestions on how to do this.)

I couldn't agree more with the young man's comments. The time has come for Catholics to take ownership of the Bible. To quote St. Paul in his second letter to the Corinthians (6:2): "NOW is the acceptable time!" As St.

Jerome once said, "Ignorance of the Scriptures is ignorance of Christ!" (*Dei Verbum*, #25). The Second Vatican Council stated firmly that "Access to sacred Scripture ought to be open wide to the Christian faithful" (*Dei Verbum*, #22). The time has come for us Catholics to embrace the gift of God's Word given to us in Holy Scripture with enthusiastic zeal and profound openness. When it comes to our approach to the Bible, we should heed the words of Deuteronomy that say, "Take to heart these words which I enjoin on you today. Drill them into your children. Speak of them at home and abroad, whether you are busy or at rest. Bind them at your wrist as a sign and let them be as a pendant on your forehead. Write them on the doorposts of your houses and on your gates" (Dt 6:6–9). Or, to put it in a form more familiar to Catholics (as we sign our forehead, lips, and breast before the gospel each week at Mass): "May the Word of God be in our minds, on our lips, and in our hearts."

Open House at God's Library: You're Invited.

God's Library is open 24 hours a day, seven days a week, 365 days a year (366 during leap years!). Your borrowing privileges are unlimited: any book for any occasion. No limit of books per customer. No overdue penalties. No need to renew your borrowing privileges...they never run out.

Plan on taking a field trip to God's Library soon...and bring a friend.

Questions for Reflection and Discussion

•What does it mean to interpret the Bible? What do we need to safeguard against interpreting the Bible recklessly?

•What are some of the different types of literature you are familiar with in the Bible?

•What does it mean that every Bible story is somehow your story?

•How will your relationship to the Bible change as a result of this book?

APPENDIX

A. Catholic Bible Study: How to Begin in Your Parish

As Catholics, our doorway to the Bible is the lectionary. The best way for Catholics to get into the habit of Bible study is to gather to read, study, share, and pray over the Scripture readings for the upcoming Sunday Mass. By doing so, we not only cover Old Testament and New Testament passages, but we also enter into the liturgical cycle and the natural rhythms that go with it. Here's how to begin:

•Gather a core group of 3 to 4 people together to meet with someone on the pastoral staff of the parish to propose your desire for Catholic Bible Study focusing on the lectionary.

•Together with someone from the pastoral staff, spend some time training two or three parishioners in the skill of *facilitating*. The facilitator is *not* a Scripture scholar or Bible expert, he or she is someone who learns the skills of moving the process along in an orderly and effective manner.

•Survey parishioners to determine a day/time/place for the study to take place. If possible, offer more than one opportunity and offer child care so that working parents can participate as well.

•Publicize well, not just in the church bulletin. Request the opportunity to offer a two-minute invitation from the pulpit after communion at all the Sunday Masses and follow up with an information table at the back of the church or in the parish center over coffee and cake.

•The format of the gatherings should be simple enough so that reliance on a staff person is kept to a minimum. Here is a suggested format:

1. Gather over refreshments for 15 minutes. Be sure to select a setting that is comfortable and hospitable…avoid classroom atmospheres.

2. The facilitator welcomes all and makes sure that all have a Bible. Arrange to provide a sufficient number of Bibles of the same translation for those who do not have one. Again, the *Revised New American Bible* is the one used in the U.S. Catholic lectionary.

3. The facilitator indicates which Sunday of the liturgical year is upcoming and which readings will be proclaimed at Mass. Participants should locate the readings in their Bible with the assistance of the facilitator and other participants. This exercise is an important part of the study. Unless we begin to discover where these readings are in the Bible, we will continue to suffer from *bibliaphobia*. Avoid using missalettes—let's get those Bibles out and start using them. Prepare scraps of paper to use as bookmarks for each of the 3 readings that are located.

4. Light a candle and put on some meditation music. Spend 3 to 5 minutes in quiet preparation to read/pray the Scripture. Option: invite all to stand and join hands in a circle and invite participants to offer out loud the prayers/petitions they bring with them. The only thing that Catholics sometimes fear more than reading the Bible is the notion of

praying out loud with others. This Bible study format should encourage Catholics to become more comfortable with both.

5. Invite one of the participants to slowly and prayerfully read the Old Testament reading for the upcoming Sunday while all follow along in their Bibles. Pause in silence after the first reading. Do the same for the New Testament letter and likewise for the gospel.

6. Arrange for participants to have a resource on hand that provides background and commentary on the Sunday Scripture readings. Together with your pastoral staff and/or diocesan Catechetical Office, you can select quality lectionary resources from a number of publishers at a reasonable cost. Spend some quiet time allowing participants the opportunity to read over the background/commentary. Option: a pastoral staff member or qualified parishioner may opt to do a brief presentation/lecture on the background/commentary. Such a lecturette may even be audio/videotaped.

7. Spend some time discussing the Scripture readings using questions provided by the resource materials that have been selected or prepared ahead of time by the facilitator. The facilitator should be sure to invite participants to offer insights and comments they have on the Scripture readings, especially life experiences that illustrate the theme of the passage being discussed. Invite any questions that participants may have. Write down questions that cannot be answered by anyone present and designate someone to research the answer with a pastoral staff member or assistance from the diocesan office.

8. The facilitator should once again invite all to stand and

join hands inviting all present to share out loud prayers of thanksgiving. A sung refrain that can be learned and led easily may be sung as a way of giving praise as well.

9. Invite participants to remain for refreshments and invite them back again for next week.

10. Be sure to continue ongoing publicity, especially inviting new parishioners and the newly initiated. Avoid taking off for the summer. Our liturgical cycle does not take a summer vacation. People will come and go on vacation as they please and crowds may grow smaller. On the other hand, moving the session to the outdoors with lawn chairs and lemonade may attract others. Arrange to provide substitutes for facilitators who will be gone for vacation.

Note: Pastors and pastoral staffs are stretched thin with numerous responsibilities. The key to this format is to train parishioners to facilitate these gatherings so that they need not rely upon the presence of a staff member at all times. Such an approach allows staff members to attend occasionally or drop in regularly. Facilitator training programs are available from a variety of publishers to teach the skills of leading discussion, prayer, and handling difficult people/situations. Contact your diocesan Catechetical Office for assistance.

B. Conducting a God's Library Workshop for Middle School and Older Young People

This workshop can be accomplished in 90 minutes and requires one adult for every 12 to 15 children. It may also be adapted for teens and adults. The workshop requires that all participants have the same version of the Bible on hand so as to assist in locating passages quickly by using page numbers. It also requires one copy of the God's Library Bookmarks (see following) and a pair of scissors for each participant.

GOAL

To build the participant's familiarity and comfort with the structure of the Bible and to increase the ease with which participants will be able to locate books, chapters, verses, and famous stories/figures in the Bible.

LEARNING OUTCOMES

Participants will be able to more easily and quickly locate biblical books, chapters, and verses using the table of contents. Likewise, participants will be able to more easily and quickly identify the location of famous stories and figures by using the God's Library Bookmarks.

ACTION PLAN

1. Be sure all participants have the same version of the Bible, preferably the New American Bible.

2. Begin by introducing the notion of how important the Bible is to us as Christians and how we are going to learn more about the Bible in this session. Ask how many have heard of the following stories (raise hands):

- David and Goliath

- Noah's ark

- Jonah and the whale

- Jesus in the Garden of Gethsemane

Most likely, all will raise their hands.

3. Next, tell participants that you will offer a prize ($1 or $5, etc.) to the first person who can find one of these stories in the Bible in 60 seconds or less. Use a stopwatch (and a whistle) and give 60 seconds for each of the 4 stories listed above, one at a time. Most likely, none will be able to do so. (If you believe your audience is more astute than this, be sure to allow only 30-45 seconds lest you go broke!)

4. Point out how unfortunate this is that we know about these stories but we don't know how to find them in the Bible. Explain that we will be working on that in this workshop.

5. Next, tell participants to have their Bible ready. Write the following biblical citations on the board (be sure to use abbreviations):

> Ez 12: 6–8
>
> Jb 2:3–11
>
> 1 Thes 5:2–4

Again, allow participants 30 to 60 seconds to locate these passages. Most will be unable to do so in the time allotted. Point out once again how unfortunate it is that we seem to be unable to identify Bible passages by their abbreviations. Ask if anyone can say out loud what the above abbreviations are.

6. Explain that if the Bible is so important to us, then we are going to need to learn how to find things in it much better and quicker. Explain that the Bible is not really a book but God's Library.

7. Explain that when you go to a library, you need to use the "catalogue" and the book numbering system to locate the book you want to read. Point out how God's Library has a "catalogue," too, namely, the Table of Contents. Have all participants open their Bible to the Table of Contents section at the beginning. Adult supervisors should assist children here. Point out the alphabetical index, the abbreviation page, and other highlights of the table of contents in your version of the Bible.

8. Using the Table of Contents, invite participants to tell you what page the following books begin on:

> Deuteronomy
>
> Judges
>
> Esther
>
> Luke

Next, using the abbreviation table, ask participants to identify which book you are referring to when you write on the board:

Hb	(Habakkuk)
Na	(Nahum)
Ti	(Titus)

9. Using the board, point out how book, chapter, and verse are used in biblical citation:

Title of Book (abbreviated) Chapter: Verse–Verse

Invite several participants to go to the board with their Bible open to the abbreviation table and write out in biblical citation the following passages as you say them:

Ecclesiastes, chapter nine, verses one to eight (Answer: Eccl 9:1–8)

Second Letter of Paul to Timothy, chapter two, verse four to six (2 Tim 2:4–6)

(Select more if you wish depending on the size of your crowd, how quickly they are catching on, and how much time you have left.)

Once again, depending upon which Bible you are using, Scripture citation may be handled differently. While most Bibles use the system described above, don't be surprised to find that some Bibles use a period or a comma instead of a colon to indicate the difference between chapter and verse. For example, The gospel of John, chapter three, verse sixteen may be found in any of the following ways depending upon which Bible you are using: Jn 3:16, Jn 3, 16 or Jn 3.16. Likewise, instead of a hyphen between verses, some Bibles will simply use a comma (Jn 3.16,18 as opposed to Jn. 3:16–18). Be sure everyone is "on the same page" with your approach to Scripture citation before you move on!

10. Now explain how to find famous stories and passages when we don't know what book, chapter, and verse they are in. Use the concept of God's Library again and draw a diagram on board (see page 15 in chapter 2). Imagine a building divided into two parts: Old Testament (Hebrew Scriptures) and New Testament (Christian Scriptures). Ask how we differentiate between these two.

Old Testament (Hebrew Scriptures): stories about the people of Israel before Jesus

New Testament (Christian Scriptures): stories about Jesus and the Christian church

Invite all participants to locate the place in the Bible where the Old Testament ends and the New Testament begins. Insert the plain bookmark here. Show how much larger the Old Testament is than the New. Ask participants what section they should be in if they are going to look for a story about Jesus.

11. Explain that in addition to breaking down the Bible into two large sections, we are now going to break it down into eight smaller sections; four in each testament. Distribute copies of the God's Library Bookmarks (see following) and a pair of scissors to each participant.

12. Beginning with the Old Testament, identify the four sections:

Pentateuch, History, Wisdom, Prophets

Have participants place one bookmark at a time, beginning with Pentateuch. Explain what can be found in this section using the information provided on the bookmark. Show from what book to what book this section entails and have participants insert the bookmark at the end of the section. Example: Pentateuch bookmark goes on the last page of Deuteronomy. Using the bookmark, point out what stories/people can be found in this section. Invite participants to locate a few. Do the same for each of the four sections of the Old Testament.

13. Do the same with each of the four sections of the New Testament:

Gospels, Acts, Letters, Revelation

Point out that while Acts and Revelation are individual books, not really a "section," it is easier to separate them this

way. Continue cutting out and inserting bookmarks one section at a time as you give a brief overview of what can be
found in each section. Encourage participants to locate
some stories as you talk about them. Spend extra time pointing out the gospel section. Ask participants to hold up the
section from Matthew through John: emphasize that if you
want to find a Jesus story, this is where to look. Remember
that all of the information you need is on the bookmarks.

14. Once all the bookmarks have been inserted, continue
drilling participants as time allows, locating famous stories
and figures in the Bible from the information provided on
the bookmarks. Award prizes (candy, etc.) for just being in
the right section (i.e. Pentateuch, Letters, etc.)

15. Encourage participants to continue doing this on their
own until they can remove the bookmarks as they would
training wheels—when they are able to locate famous stories and figures within just a few minutes by knowing which
section to look for. Encourage participants to show their
parents, friends, pastor, etc., how they have learned to find
their way around the Bible with such ease and familiarity.

Bible Table of
Contents/Abbreviation Page

Old Testament

Genesis	Gn	Job	Jb
Exodus	Ex	Psalms	Ps
Leviticus	Lv	Proverbs	Prv
Numbers	Nm	Ecclesiastes	Eccl
Deuteronomy	Dt	Song of Songs	Sg
Joshua	Jos	Wisdom	Wis
Judges	Jgs	Sirach	Sir
Ruth	Ru	Isaiah	Is
1 Samuel	1Sm	Jeremiah	Jer
2 Samuel	2Sm	Lamentations	Lam
1 Kings	1Kgs	Baruch	Bar
2 Kings	2Kgs	Ezekiel	Ez
1 Chronicles	1Chr	Daniel	Dn
2 Chronicles	2Chr	Hosea	Hos
Ezra	Ez	Joel	Jl
Nehemiah	Neh	Amos	Am
Tobit	Tb	Obadiah	Ob
Judith	Jdt	Jonah	Jon
Esther	Est	Micah	Mi
1 Maccabees	1Mac	Nahum	Na
2 Maccabees	2Mac	Habakkuk	Hb
Zephaniah	Zep	Haggai	Hg
Zechariah	Zec	Malachi	Mal

New Testament

Matthew	Mt	2 Thessalonians	2Thes
Mark	Mk	1 Timothy	1Tim
Luke	Lk	2 Timothy	2Tim
John	Jn	Titus	Ti
Acts of the Apostles	Acts	Philemon	Phlm
Romans	Rom	Hebrews	Heb
1 Corinthians	1Cor	James	Jas
2 Corinthians	1Cor	1 Peter	1Pt
Galatians	Gal	2 Peter	2Pt
Ephesians	Eph	1 John	1Jn
Philippians	Phil	2 John	2Jn
Colossians	Col	3 John	3Jn
1 Thessalonians	1Thes	Jude	Jude
		Revelation	Rv

Alphabetical

Old Testament

Amos	Am	1Kings	1Kgs
Baruch	Bar	2 Kings	2Kgs
1 Chronicles	1Chr	Lamentations	Lam
2 Chronicles	2Chr	Leviticus	Lv
Daniel	Dn	1 Maccabees	1Mac
Deuteronomy	Dt	2 Maccabees	2Mac
Ecclesiastes	Eccl	Malachi	Mal
Esther	Est	Micah	Mi
Exodus	Ex	Nahum	Na
Ezra	Ezr	Nehemiah	Neh
Ezekiel	Ez	Numbers	Nm
Genesis	Gn	Obadiah	Ob
Habakkuk	Hb	Proverbs	Prv
Haggai	Hg	Psalms	Ps
Hosea	Hos	Ruth	Ru
Isaiah	Is	1 Samuel	1Sm
Jeremiah	Jer	2 Samuel	2Sm
Job	Jb	Sirach	Sir
Joel	Jl	Song of Songs	Sg
Jonah	Jon	Tobit	Tb
Joshua	Jos	Wisdom	Wis
Judges	Jgs	Zechariah	Zec
Judith	Jdt	Zephaniah	Zep

New Testament

Acts of the Apostles	Acts
Colossians	Col
1 Corinthians	1Cor
2 Corinthians	2Cor
Ephesians	Eph
Galatians	Gal
Hebrews	Heb
James	Jas
John (Gospel)	Jn
1 John	1Jn
2 John	2Jn
3 John	3Jn
Jude	Jude
Luke	Lk
Mark	Mk
Matthew	Mt
1 Peter	1Pt
2 Peter	2Pt
Philemon	Phlm
Philippians	Phil
Revelation	Rev
Romans	Rom
1 Thessalonians	1Thes
2 Thessalonians	2Thes
1 Timothy	1Tm
2 Timothy	2Tm
Titus	Ti

Bibliography

Charpentier, Etienne. *How to Read the Old Testament* (New York: Crossroad Publishing Company, 1992).

Witherington III, Ben. *Conflict & Community in Corinth: A Socio-Rhetorical Commentary on 1 and 2 Corinthians* (Grand Rapids, MI: Wm. B. Eerdmans Publishing Co. and Carlisle, Cumbria, U.K.: The Paternoster Press, 1995).

Brown, S.S., Raymond E., Joseph A. Fitzmyer, S.J., Roland E. Murphy, O. Carm., Editors. *The Jerome Biblical Commentary* (Englewood Cliffs, NJ: Prentice-Hall, 1968).

Ludwig, Robert A. *Reconstructing Catholicism: For a New Generation* (New York: Crossroad Publishing Company, 1995).

The Pontifical Biblical Commission. *The Interpretation of the Bible in the Church,* printed in *Origins* (January 6, 1994, Vol. 23: No. 29).

Dei Verbum, Dogmatic Constitution on Divine Revelation, 18 Nov. 1965, *Vatican Council II: The Conciliar and Post Conciliar Documents*, Austin Flannery, OP, General Editor (Collegeville, MN: Liturgical Press, 1975).

Bergant, C.S.A., Dianne. *Introduction to the Bible*, Collegeville Bible Commentary (Collegeville, MN: Liturgical Press, 1985).

The Complete Parallel Bible (NRSV, REB, NAB, NJB) (New York/Oxford: Oxford University Press, 1993).

The New American Bible (Nashville/ New York: Thomas Nelson, Publishers, 1971).

The Catholic Bible: Personal Study Edition. New American Bible with Revised NT (New York/Oxford: Oxford University Press, 1995).

PENTATEUCH

(Genesis through Deuteronomy)

Place this bookmark on the last page of the book of Deuteronomy. Welcome to the section called the "Pentateuch", or "Torah" meaning the five books of the Law. This section captures the beginnings of the relationship between God and the people of Israel with the central focus being the Exodus event...the experience of being led from slavery to freedom. Here are some of the highlights:

- the creation stories
- Adam and Eve
- Cain and Abel
- Noah's ark
- The tower of Babel
- Sodom and Gomorrah
- Abraham and Sarah
- Isaac and Rebekah
- Jacob and Esau
- Joseph (the "coat of many colors")
- Moses (in the reeds, the burning bush, the ten plagues, crossing of the Red Sea, the Passover, the ten commandments, the ark of the covenant, journey through the desert, death of Moses)
- the twelve tribes of Israel
- the laws, traditions, and feasts of Israel

HISTORY

(Joshua through 2nd Maccabees)

Place this bookmark on the last page of 2 Maccabees. You've now entered the History section of God's Library...the section that records the story of the people of Israel fighting to establish and keep the promised land under various leaders (judges and kings). Here are the highlights:

- Joshua (crossing the Jordan, the walls of Jericho)
- Samson and Delilah
- Ruth and Naomi
- Samuel (request for a king)
- King Saul
- David and Goliath, King David
- Solomon (the Temple, Queen of Sheba)
- Elijah and Elisha
- many kings, battles, and genealogies
- division of the kingdom
- exile and return
- Judith and Esther

WISDOM

(Job through Sirach)

Place this bookmark at the end of the book of Sirach. You're now ready to explore the Wisdom section of the Bible. While the Bible contains wisdom throughout, this section collects all of the wisdom of the people of Israel collected over thousands of years of wandering the desert, living in the promised land, worshiping in the temple, and struggling through exile. Among the many anecdotes, sayings, prayers, poems, and songs, here are some highlights:

- Job's suffering
- 150 Psalms for all occasions
- hundreds of proverbs
- wise sayings including "Vanity of vanities, all things are vanity!" and "There is a time for everything" and "A faithful friend is a sturdy shelter" and more
- a romantic love song
- thousands more sayings about wisdom, prudence, good health, wealth, holiness, family, friends, misery, death, and even table etiquette.

PROPHETS

(Isaiah through Malachi)

Place this at the end of the book of Malachi (which also coincides with the bookmark separating the Old and New Testaments). Welcome to the last section of the Old Testament: the Prophets. The prophets were not concerned with foretelling the future, but with calling the people of Israel back to their past fidelity to God, lest they face doom. Likewise, they held out hope for the future when the people of Israel found themselves doomed in exile. From this hope comes the notion of a messiah and an everlasting kingdom. Yet, even these assurances of a future are based on a return to the fidelity of the past. Here are some highlights:

The "major" (lengthier) prophets Isaiah (Immanuel, "the people who walked in darkness have seen a great light," "comfort my people," etc.
Jeremiah (call of Jeremiah, exile and return)
Ezekiel (the dry bones)

The "minor" (shorter) prophets Daniel (the lion's den, Shadrach, Meshach, and Abednego)
Jonah (swallowed by a whale)
…and more.

GOSPELS

(Matthew, Mark, Luke, and John)

Place this bookmark at the end of the Gospel of John and prepare to enter the part of God's Library where we walk with Jesus. The Gospels contain the stories that are most sacred to our Christian faith and heritage: the life, teachings, miracles, passion, death, and resurrection of Jesus of Nazareth. Here are some highlights:

- the birth of Jesus
- the Holy Family (Mary and Joseph)
- the finding in the temple
- temptation in the desert and the baptism of Jesus
- the Beatitudes and the Our Father
- parables (the prodigal son, the good samaritan, the sower, etc.)
- the golden rule
- numerous miracles (calming of the storm, healing of the blind, deaf, and paralyzed, raising of Lazarus, changing water into wine, feeding 5000, walking on water, etc.)
- the last supper, the eucharist, and the washing of the feet
- the agony in the garden
- Peter's denial and Judas' betrayal
- the way of the cross and crucifixion
- Resurrection and appearances
- dozens of fascinating characters: Zacchaeus, Mary Magdelene, Nicodemus, the Samaritan woman, Martha and Mary, etc.
- powerful images such as the Bread of Life, the Light of the World, the Way, Truth, and the Life

ACTS OF THE APOSTLES

(One book only: the Acts of the Apostles)

This section of the Bible is easy because it is just one book: the Acts of the Apostles. Place your bookmark at the end of this book and visit the experience of the early Christian community. In many ways, the book of Acts is a sequel to the Gospels, especially the Gospel of Luke since both were written by the same author. Here are some highlights of the Acts:

- Jesus' ascension
- the descent of the Holy Spirit on Pentecost
- descriptions of the communal life of the early church
- Stephen's martyrdom
- Philip and the Ethiopian
- Saul's conversion and baptism
- the missionary work of Peter, Saul (Paul), Barnabas, and others
- miracles at the hands of Peter and Paul
- Paul's travels, imprisonment, trials, shipwreck, and arrival in Rome

(Permission is granted to photocopy bookmarks for personal use)

THE LETTERS (Epistles)

(Romans through Jude)

Place this bookmark at the end of the letter of Jude. Welcome to the communications of the early church, before there were e-mail, phones, and FAXes. Of the 21 letters, also known as epistles, the majority (12) are attributed to Paul. These letters are addressed to communities of Christians and to the leaders of these communities and were designed to teach, admonish, encourage, correct, and update the various churches. Here are some highlights:

Paul: theology, teachings, and exhortations concerning:
- grace
- justification by faith
- the Law
- the Eucharist
- the metaphor of the Body
- variety and unity of gifts
- ministry
- suffering
- Christ and his cross
- Christian conduct

James: faith and good works, anointing of the sick

1 John: "Beloved, let us love one another..."

REVELATION

(One book only, the Book of Revelation/the Apocalpyse)

Place your last bookmark at the end of the book of Revelation and you've reached the end of the Bible! As you enter the book of Revelation, be aware that it is one of the most misunderstood books of the Bible. Many falsely use this book to predict the end of the world. Written in "apocalyptic" language, the book of Revelation uses many symbols and figurative language to describe the eternal struggle between good and evil. Despite all of the frightening imagery, the uplifting conclusion of this book is that GOOD HAS AND WILL ALWAYS PREVAIL! Here are the highlights:

- visions and messages to the seven churches
- the scroll and the lamb
- the 144,000 saved
- the seven trumpets
- the woman and the dragon
- the King of Kings
- the Thousand-Year Reign
- the new heavens and new earth
- the new Jerusalem
- "Come, Lord Jesus!"

(Permission is granted to photocopy bookmarks for personal use)

Also by Joe Paprocki

Tools for Teaching
Classroom Tips for Catechists

A do-it-yourself manual with instructions for approaching a wide variety of cate-chetical challenges: planning lessons, handling discipline problems, using text-books and teacher manuals, praying with your class, choosing appropriate student activities, and more. A great companion for new catechists, a great refresher for veterans. 128 pp, $7.95 (order B-33)

Seven Steps to Great Religion Classes
with Gwen Costello

A step by step look at seven important elements of a great religion class: the process of lesson planning; skills needed to create a positive environment; strate-gies for motivating children; techniques for maintaining and handling discipline; and more. Each chapter includes reflection and discussion questions and a con-cluding prayer. 80 pp, $7.95 (order C-09)

On video
Welcome to God's Library
Introducing Catholics to the Bible

Are you one of those Catholics who suffer from "bibliaphobia" (fear of the Bible)? Do you feel ill-at-ease with the parts of the Bible, with the unusual names and places, some of the images and incredible events it contains? In this videotape Joe Paprocki compares reading the Bible to entering a library filled with books of var-ious genre. By understanding the organization of the Bible and how to use its components, the reader can become more comfortable with it and discover where and how to locate key figures, stories, and passages. The tape provides a session outline for a God's Library Workshop, which is a wonderfully helpful experience both for children and adults.

This must-have for catechists, teachers, RCIA coordinators, and pastoral min-isters is a perfect compliment to the *God's Library* book.

approx. 43 minutes, $29.95 (order A-46)

Available at religious bookstores or from:

TWENTY-THIRD PUBLICATIONS

PO BOX 180 · 185 WILLOW STREET ⊛ MYSTIC, CT 06355 · 1-800-321-0411
FAX: 1-800-572-0788 BAYARD E-MAIL: ttpubs@aol.com

Use this bookmark
to separate the
Old Testament
from the
New Testament

(Permission is granted to photocopy bookmarks for personal use)